Praise for

The Jesus Plan

"A radical call to move 'outside the box' of traditional thinking regarding the function and structure of the church. Dreisbach's approach to church growth is biblically balanced and relationally centered, is documented by insightful research, and is lavishly illustrated by practical examples and life situations. Refreshingly relevant and candidly honest, *The Jesus Plan* is must-reading for all who care to find a workable, Spirit-led solution to the status quo and malaise afflicting much of today's church."

—MARVIN R. WILSON, author and professor
of biblical studies at Gordon College

"With fascinating descriptions of his own experience, Dreisbach helps us understand why so many people find the church irrelevant. He then proceeds to outline an approach whereby Christians can build relationships with those whose thinking and lifestyle may be entirely outside any church context. The result is that the gospel gets a fresh hearing, people do find that Jesus Christ is relevant, and they discover how to live redemptively under His direction."

—DONALD H. GILL, church consultant and former
president of Vision New England

"This small volume helps dispel the fears of the average Christian toward sharing their faith. Elegant in its simplicity, this is a fresh vision for every pastor and layperson who understand evangelism to be one of the primary goals of every congregation and every Christ-follower."

—RAYMOND F. PENDLETON, PH.D., chair, division of The Ministry
of the Church, Gordon-Conwell Theological Seminary

"What is the price of a soul? Bruce not only reminds us of God's heart for the lost, he makes us question our own hearts: Am I willing to pay the price for the lost souls in my life? Have I forgotten the lost because I am found? *The Jesus Plan* enables us to confidently share our lives and our faith with those God has placed in our lives. It reignited my own passion to reach one more for eternity."

—SHARON DIETRICH, Community Bible Study Teaching Director,
Conference and Retreat Speaker

the JESUS PLAN

the JESUS PLAN

BREAKING THROUGH BARRIERS
TO INTRODUCE THE PEOPLE YOU KNOW
TO THE GOD YOU LOVE

BRUCE ROBERTS DREISBACH

WATERBROOK
PRESS

THE JESUS PLAN
PUBLISHED BY WATERBROOK PRESS
2375 Telstar Drive, Suite 160
Colorado Springs, Colorado 80920
A division of Random House, Inc.

ISBN 1-57856-435-2

Library of Congress Cataloging-in-Publication Data
Dreisbach, Bruce Roberts.
    The Jesus Plan : breaking through barriers to introduce the people you know
    to the God you love / Bruce Roberts Dreisbach.—1st ed.
        p. cm.
    ISBN 1-57856-435-2
    1. Evangelistic work—United States. I. Title.

BV3790 .D72 2001
269'.2'0973—dc21

2001046788

Printed in the United States of America
2002—First Edition

10 9 8 7 6 5 4 3 2 1

To the three beautiful women in my life:
Martie, Katybeth, and Megan

CONTENTS

ACKNOWLEDGMENTS

This book reflects the wisdom and combined experience of the hundreds, if not thousands, of people who have each contributed to the development of the New Life Ministry and the growing movement of new-paradigm churches in America. In reality, I stand as a scribe rather than an architect of this new expression of the church God has raised up to reach the lost in our day and age. For the many and varied contributions of each, I am profoundly grateful.

Dave Morgan has been my partner in ministry for almost thirty years. Not only did he coauthor the creation of New Life, he served as the first leader of both our local ministry and our initial efforts to train others across the United States in developing New Life for their communities. Our teaching team (Steve and Christie Bravo, Peter and Allison Balentine, Dave Morgan, and myself) created most of the principles and training ideas of New Life, many of which are described in this volume. I am grateful for their hard work and perseverance over many years.

I cannot begin to express my gratitude to the people who were the first to take a risk and commit themselves to becoming New Life missionaries to lost family and friends. Your willingness to try a new way of reaching the lost has allowed God to do "the new thing" He desires to redeem many for Christ.

Stephanie Taylor and Jennifer Cruz began this book in the early days of the ministry. Carol Smith has carried the ball in providing production support to my writing efforts over the past four years. Thank you for working your way through all my handwritten scrawl, typing and retyping, offering positive suggestions, and, in so many ways, turning my thoughts into useful resources. I'm amazed at how you manage to make me look good!

My sincere thanks to Thomas Womack and the entire team at Water-Brook Press. I'm grateful for your faith in this issue and your willingness to take on this unknown author. Thank you for blowing on the coals and fanning the flames of my passion for lost people during the long process on the way to publication.

Finally, I could not have written this book nor developed this ministry without the love and support of my wife, Martie, and our two children, Katybeth and Megan. As in all the good God has done in my life, they are prime creators and coauthors. Thank you for your ideas, your challenges, your encouragement, and your love. Together as we walk with Jesus, we will continue to discover what it is to be ambassadors for Christ, disturbers of the universe.

INTRODUCTION

Life is precious. Especially spiritual life. If you're a follower of Jesus Christ, you know that. Many of us have forgotten what it feels like to be lost, without hope in this world or the next. My desire is that this book will connect you again with those feelings and stimulate genuine compassion for the lost people who surround us.

On average, six or seven of every ten people in our world are spiritually lost. They're people we work with each day, they're neighbors, they're extended family members. Some are even members of our immediate family—our children, grandchildren, brothers, sisters, parents. These are people we know and care about.

But for the most part, we simply don't know how to share our faith with them in a way that will make sense. And most of the spiritually lost are simply outside the reach of our local churches. They're not going to come into our churches to find God, and most traditional churches are not going to go out into the world to search for them.

This problem has been identified and discussed for a number of years. And God's solution to the problem is now becoming clear: He wants to raise up individuals and groups of people who are willing and *able* to go out and find lost people. And He has given us simple and direct ways to accomplish this.

The Jesus Plan tells the story of how God has been teaching some of my friends and me to reach these lost people. We simply want to share with you what He's taught us. My prayer is that these insights will offer as much hope to you as they have to us.

These methods work. They are working right now in our own start-up ministries in other cities as well as in many other breakout, new-paradigm churches across America. And they can also work for you and for your friends.

As we view the church as God's means for fulfilling the Great Commission—for going out, finding the lost, leading them to faith in Christ, and discipling them to spiritual maturity—it's clear what this new approach to evangelism offers. It is relationally driven and works through communities and networks of people to achieve God's objectives. In our postmodern, post-Christian culture, these relational strategies are effective in reaching people who won't come to church. We may think of the strategies as new, but they look a lot like the early church's approach in the first three centuries after Christ. At that time the world was a pluralistic, secular culture that was often anti-Christian—a lot like the world you and I live in at the beginning of the twenty-first century.

Lost people matter greatly to God. He loves them desperately and wants us to work with Him as He rescues and redeems these lost ones and brings them into His family.

Invite Him to help you reach the people you care about.

CHAPTER 1

LOST

———

With a growing sense of panic, the truth became clear to me: I was lost. I had no idea where I was in those woods or how to get out safely. And darkness was setting in.

Having broken a cardinal rule of woodcraft, I realized I was in deep trouble. It was my fault, and now I was trapped. As I thought about the possible consequences, feelings of fear and helplessness swept over me.

The day had started so well. My new bride and I were living in a suburb of Boston. An avid outdoorsman, I loved to explore the beautiful New England countryside to find new places to hike and fish. On this splendid, crisp October Saturday, I'd driven to Middlesex County in Massachusetts to sample the noted trout fishing on the Squannacook River. I reached the quaint village of Groton—home of the famous Yankee prep school of the same name—then drove for several miles outside town and parked where a narrow road led into the woods. From looking at the map, I guessed that this road cut back to the Squannacook. I gathered up my tackle and lunch and hiked in.

Soon the road became overgrown and eventually narrowed to just a path. Finally, the path itself faded out into undifferentiated woodland.

As a youngster, I'd been a Boy Scout, and in college, I taught woodcraft and survival skills for the Boy Scouts. I knew never to leave a path in strange terrain without a compass and a topographic map. But I could almost hear the river just beyond the trees ahead. I was sure I was very close. How much farther could it be?

Well, it was farther than I expected, but I finally bushwhacked my way to the banks of the Squannacook. I had a great morning, catching a number of beautiful native brook trout. After lunch, a short nap, and an afternoon of more fishing, I was ready to go home.

Heading back upstream, I kept looking for the spot where I'd first reached the river. But each section of woods and underbrush looked remarkably similar. Several times I started into the woods on what I thought was the path back to the road, but I ended up confused. Nothing looked familiar.

At one point in the woods, I reached swampy ground. I was dumbfounded. I had seen no swamp on my way in! I thrashed through the knee-deep bog, totally disoriented, and I began thinking of people I'd known who had died in the woods from such foolish mistakes.

The sun was about to set. I decided that going back and following the river was my only chance to survive. I again worked my way out of the woods to the riverbank. I followed the stream's course, past wide sections too deep to wade across.

Then, beyond the woods on the other side, I heard a car pass by! I picked the narrowest point in the river I could find, clamped my fly rod in my jaws, and proceeded to swim across the forty-yard expanse of frigid water. My clothes, my tackle, and my hiking boots tried to drag me under. Thankfully, I made it through the powerful current and pulled myself out, exhausted and shivering, on the opposite bank.

A short hike through the woods brought me out to a secondary blacktop road. I picked a direction and hoped it would lead to town.

Darkness was settling in, and it was getting colder and colder. After walking several miles on the dark, quiet road in my soaking clothes and boots, I finally arrived back at my car. I was grateful to have survived at all. I sat in my car shivering, but I was happy to be on my way home.

A GREATER LOSTNESS

Lost in the woods—that was me on that October evening. It's also an accurate description of my spiritual condition earlier as a young adult. Perhaps my description of confusion, fear, panic, and even terror induced by my misguided adventure along the Squannacook can help you understand how I felt growing up with no knowledge of God—and how others feel who are spiritually lost today.

I was raised in the sixties in a nice Philadelphia suburb in a typical middle-class home. My family was essentially unchurched, though my mother occasionally attended the local Quaker Meeting where she was a member. My father never went along—to him, I think, not going to church was a strongly held religious principle. We kids dropped out of the process altogether by third grade. My parents made several half-hearted attempts to teach us values or morality or religion, but without much effect.

Until I was in the fifth grade, we stood up every day at my public elementary school and recited the Lord's Prayer along with the Pledge of Allegiance. The teachers just seemed to assume we all knew what the prayer meant, but I was clueless, and no one ever bothered to explain. I just mumbled along with the rest of the class. And although many of the other kids were from families of committed churchgoers, I never heard anyone talk about having a relationship with Jesus or what difference it could make.

As a teenager I became deeply immersed in rock music. I'd been in the sixth grade when the Beatles first landed in America and appeared on *The Ed Sullivan Show*. I can associate the release of every subsequent Beatles album with my grade in school plus a variety of events, activities, and people I was involved with at the time.

My friends had rock bands and practiced in their garages at home, and everyone dreamed of becoming the next Jim Morrison or Janis Joplin. At night we hunkered down in a place where our parents couldn't hear and listened to the latest songs on WMMR, the underground rock station out of Philly.

When I was seventeen, we heard about a summer concert out in the country with performers from the underground rock scene. My buddies Jack and Mark and I piled into an Olds 88 that Mark's family owned and headed north. About two and a half hours from home we pulled into an old pasture and found a place to pitch our tent between the dried-up cow patties. People kept coming and coming. Two days later it became clear that this little Woodstock gathering of rock bands and music fans on Max Yasgur's farm was destined to become historic.

My Search Begins

It was during those teen years that I began seriously considering my purpose in life and searching for what I wanted to get out of it. Seeing the world only through the eyes of popular culture and television, however, I had little foundation to build on.

Though alcohol was the most prominent drug of choice in my high school, I never found much satisfaction in getting drunk—try as I might. Drugs also did little to answer my ultimate questions. During this era of free love and the advent of the pill, the world around me placed a high value on sexual experiences, and I got involved with girls. But the relationships never seemed to last long or grow into something meaningful. I thought seriously about the value of education, but I couldn't tell that it made much difference for anyone. The people I knew who were well educated had no more happiness than those who weren't. They all seemed equally miserable.

As my search continued, I got involved in the fine arts scene. On weekends I rode the train into Philadelphia and hung out in Rittenhouse Square with the artsy set—many of them suburban hippies like myself trying to identify with something, anything, that was different and promised some hope of breaking out of the bleakness. We spent hours rapping with one another, discussing existential philosophy and Jack Kerouac and Ayn Rand. We tried expressing alternative values through poetry, sculpture, and painting.

At times I even looked to religion. I met a guy in the square who told me about a little Buddhist shrine I could buy. He said if I took it home and chanted before it twice a day, all my deepest desires would come true. You didn't even have to believe in the process, he said; you just had to do it. I trudged off to some grungy apartment in an alley behind Race Street and spent ten dollars on my own shrine. I tried the routine for a while, but it didn't seem to make much difference.

In my hometown, I met some Holy Rollers. On Friday nights they joined the many teenagers cruising the streets. Their goal was to buttonhole others and get them to consider the claims of Christ and to attend an evangelism service at their church in a rundown neighborhood on the edge of town. I went with them to the service a few times. I thought if I was willing to give Buddha a try, it wouldn't hurt to do the same with Christ. But I never figured out what these people were talking about. They used a lot of language I didn't understand—what was all this about blood, righteousness, and Ebenezers? Their message seemed to have no connection to reality.

AWAY FROM HOME

Meanwhile, like many teens, I found my parents' home an increasingly difficult place to be. My solution was to run away, at least for the summers. The summer I turned sixteen, I lived under the boardwalk in

Ocean City, New Jersey. I earned my food by panhandling, a skill I had learned during earlier escapes to downtown Philly.

I made a number of friends in Ocean City. One was a cheerful young black man who worked as a cook in a restaurant. He also cleaned up after the restaurant closed and the rest of the staff went home for the night. I'd show up at one o'clock in the morning and help him sweep and clean in exchange for all the leftover food I could eat or carry out.

Then I would crawl under the boardwalk—down at the end by Twenty-third Street, where the police didn't bother to patrol—dig a hole in the sand to get out of the wind, and roll up in the thin blanket I carried in my knapsack. The next morning, when the first bike-riders shook sand down between the boards into my face, I got up and started a new day of adventures.

One evening I tried to pick up a cute girl sitting on a bench looking out at the waves. We struck up a conversation, and she started talking about Jesus and having a relationship with God. Moffit, like me, was from a middle-class suburban home, but she was a good churchgoing girl. She said she'd entered into a personal relationship with Jesus the year before.

My conversation with Moffit continued off and on over the next two weeks as I kept running into her. She seemed as interested in finding out what a "hippie poet" like me thought about God as she was in sharing her own faith in Jesus. From our talks, I felt I was making some progress in understanding the God thing.

One morning in the house where she and her parents lived, Moffit told me, "It's like this, Bruce. When you look in the mirror at your life, what do you see? If you like what's there—fine, no problem. You're on your own. If you look in the mirror and don't like what you see, you can give your life to Jesus. He'll keep all the good things in your life. The bad things He'll throw out, and He'll replace them with His good things."

As I left her house and walked down the street, I glanced in the mirror at my life. I really didn't like what I saw. So I knelt there on the sidewalk and gave my life to Jesus Christ.

That was over thirty years ago, and I'm still walking with Him. And He's still in the process of tossing out the bad things of my life and replacing them with His good things.

MAKING SENSE OF MY STORY

Looking back, I sometimes wonder how I got saved at all. Rather than the result of someone's God-driven strategy to search for the lost, it's almost as if God found me by accident. I believe in God's sovereignty, so I'm not questioning how He can and does use all kinds of mysterious means to accomplish His will. Yet my experience still seems so random, so one-off—more like the first cave man who "discovered" fire simply because a lightning bolt landed next to him in the woods and set the brush ablaze.

My conversion was divine intervention. God was going to get hold of my life regardless. His grace, pure and simple—no other explanation does justice to it.

But why did it take so much miraculous effort on His part? Some of the reasons why I ended up so terribly lost had to do with wrong choices I made. Seeking meaning and satisfaction from alcohol, drugs, and sex were clearly immoral choices. Meanwhile, trying to find purpose in life from secular values, art, and education represented errors of direction on my part—they were the kinds of choices that continue to be not only socially acceptable but also strongly promoted by American culture as valid guideposts for the journey through life.

And as for the different religious choices available to me, it's no great surprise that I was confused by all of them. Many people today have trouble sorting out the truth from among the competing denominations, doctrines, self-made sects, and New Age religions. Even Christians seem confused at times about the difference between religion and a relationship with Jesus. Far too often we've exchanged the life-giving personal relationship with our Lord and Savior for a sorry mess of lifeless religious traditions and nonsense.

So how can we clear up the picture in a way that helps us effectively reach out to others who are lost?

TWO HUNDRED
MILLION

Jon Krakauer's *Into the Wild* tells the story of Chris McCandless, a recent college graduate from a well-to-do family. McCandless gave his entire life savings of $25,000 to charity and abandoned his car and most of his possessions, then hitchhiked to Alaska in April of 1992 and walked alone into the wilderness. His earnest desire was to learn to live off the land to find meaning, purpose, and direction for his life.

Four months later, a moose hunter found McCandless's decomposed body back in the Alaskan bush.

This chilling and fascinating story of good intentions and unbelievably bad consequences is an apt parable about the spiritually lost in America today. Being lost is not their intentional decision. Many, like McCandless, have quite admirable intentions for their journey in life. But things don't work out as they hoped. Many become increasingly lost because they don't have critical information, or the information they've been given is simply untrue. Others make mistakes of judgment or simply make wrong choices. Often no one's around to offer help when they finally realize they're confused, disoriented, and way over their heads in trouble.

They're lost! All too often, like Chris McCandless, before they can get help and change their course, it's too late. They've made a series of choices that prove to be fatal...forever. No matter what the reasons, each of these people stands in grave danger of spending eternity shut out from the presence of a loving heavenly Father.

Millions of Americans today are lost. They're lost not only spiritually but in many other ways. They're relationally lost, with marriages, families, and friendships in terminal forms of dysfunction. They're emotionally and psychologically lost, embroiled in deep wounds and damaging patterns from which there seems to be no relief. They're lost in terms of having no sense of community, as they live in a culture where the extended family has been washed away by migration patterns in which the average American family moves once every five years. Nuclear families have been destroyed by divorce. And well over half the children in schools today are survivors of a broken home.

Researchers indicate as many as two hundred million men, women, and children are among those lost in America today. Put another way, as many as seven out of ten of the people you know are in grave danger. Like Chris McCandless, they've wandered off into the woods and face imminent peril from death.

Many of them are people we work with at the office every day. They may be friends and acquaintances we see at the health club or at our kids' athletic events. They may be neighbors with whom we've talked off and on for years. They could even be members of our extended family or living in our own home. They are people of different ages and stages in life, with different needs and concerns. People who have ended up thoroughly lost for a variety of reasons—yet who all face the same terrifying prospect of spending life and eternity outside the loving home of God.

All So Different

In the classic children's tale *Peter Pan,* Wendy and her brothers fly to Neverland to discover Peter's secret world. Peter is the leader of a band of characters who call themselves the Lost Boys. They've been separated from their families and have ended up in Neverland in a tribe of similarly displaced peers.

But as Wendy gets to know them, she discovers a great deal of variation in the boys' attitudes. Some are independent, while others long so much for the care and nurture of parents that they "adopt" Wendy as their "mother." Several exhibit a variety of dysfunctions that have inhibited their maturation. Many feel quite badly about being separated from their families; others hold firmly to rebellious disobedience. While all the Lost Boys share the same fate in Neverland until they're found, the similarities end there.

The same is true of the spiritually lost today. Many actually grew up in churchgoing families and have no idea where they took the wrong turn that landed them deep in a dismal swamp. While some are hardened, ingrained in a life of disobedience, rebelliousness, and sin, many others have a tremendous yearning for something more than their secular worldview offers them. Many others have become so dysfunctional from the wrong choices they've continually made that they can no longer even search for a way out. Their lives have collapsed into a vicious downward spiral of disastrous choices and consequences.

Some realize they're lost, and if they knew how to get out of the woods and find God, they would act on that knowledge. But they don't know how. That's the essence of being lost.

Many more aren't even aware they're lost. They believe much of what they've been told—that the American Dream leads to heaven or the equivalent thereof. Or that some other false god or value can provide them with all they want from life.

ONE EXAMPLE

Jason Patterson was raised in a Catholic family on the North Shore of Massachusetts. He made what he believed to be a commitment of faith as a child of eight or ten, but as he grew older he fell away from the Lord and the church. He moved south and embarked on a successful business career. He rose to success and prominence as an executive for a large firm in Delaware and had a wonderful wife and great kids.

In many ways the world around him was telling Jason he was an enormous success—a winner. Others aspired to be like him. In his midfifties he found himself wealthy and powerful. But inside he felt a gnawing emptiness, a hunger for something he didn't have. It wasn't material. It wasn't social or recreational.

Jason was lost. Finally, after a number of wrong choices and misguided attempts to find a way out of his lost condition, he experienced an explosion of negative consequences in his life, including a broken marriage and rejection by his family. Every good accomplishment he'd ever made, all his hard work in the right areas, was being consumed in a fireball of painful consequences.

Jason didn't intend to get lost. For most of his life, while he was drifting farther from God and sinking deeper in the swamp, he was being praised for leading such a successful life. Yet here he was, terrified and expecting the worst, knowing his pain was self-inflicted but having no idea how to find help or a way out of his predicament.

Even worse than what he knew about his situation was what he didn't know. He was in danger of losing everything in eternity as well as in this life.

HOW DOES GOD SEE THEM?

How does God feel about someone like Jason? How does He view these millions of our friends, neighbors, coworkers, and family members who are lost in America?

Scripture is very clear—*lost people matter to God!* Jesus told us, "Your Father in heaven is not willing that any of these little ones should be lost" (Matthew 18:14). The Bible is full of stories that show the compassion of God for lost people and the incredible efforts the Father is willing to go to to redeem them.

In Luke 15, Jesus used three stories to tell us that lost people matter to God even as much as a lost child would matter to you or me. What would you do if one of your children didn't come home from school one afternoon? Would you simply shrug your shoulders and say, "He'll turn up eventually. Say, what's for dinner?" Of course you wouldn't. You would start calling your child's friends. You would get in your car and scour the neighborhood. You would call the police. You would get helpers to comb the nearby woods and fields. You would search and pray and search some more. There's probably no effort or expense you would spare until your lost child was found.

That's exactly how God feels about each one of the lost people in our world today. He'll spare no effort or expense to find even one of these lost ones in this world He created.

God proved His love when He sent and sacrificed His only Son, Jesus, in order to save the lost in this world. He would have made that supreme sacrifice even if there were only one who was lost—it could have been you or me. Lost people matter that much to God.

WRONG ASSUMPTIONS?

We need to pray that God will break our hearts and our proud spirits that we might see these two hundred million lost souls in the same way He does. Our own response to the lost should reflect the compassion felt by our Father in heaven. As biblical Christians, the plight of the vast majority of Americans should alarm us to the point of action.

But in this world of lost and hurting people, we aren't going to reach them simply by going through the motions or practicing business as usual.

So what exactly should our action be?

In Matthew 10 the twelve disciples were "sent out" by Jesus (verse 5) after being given authority "to drive out evil spirits and to heal every disease and sickness" (verse 1). Luke 10 records Jesus sending out seventy-two disciples as He told them, "The harvest is plentiful, but the workers are few" (verse 2). Before ascending into heaven, the resurrected Christ told His followers, "All authority in heaven and on earth has been given to me. Therefore *go and make disciples of all nations*" (Matthew 28:18-19), and "You will receive power when the Holy Spirit comes on you; and you will be my witnesses *in Jerusalem, and in all Judea and Samaria, and to the ends of the earth*" (Acts 1:8).

The conclusion is inescapable. *We must be willing to go out and search for the lost* so that God can redeem them. God Himself is asking—no, commanding—those of us who love Him to go out into the dark night and comb the woods until these lost ones are found and brought into the family of God.

But in our approach to seeking the lost, Christians too often have been making a lot of assumptions that simply aren't true. We use a style of ministry based on a world and society that no longer exist. America has gone through incredible transformation in recent decades, while we inside the church soldier on, using decades-old outreach methods. Then we wonder why these "proven," "biblical," and "traditional" methods no longer seem to be as fruitful as they once were.

The purpose of this book is to help us examine our assumptions about the world we live in today and determine how to go about accomplishing what God has called us to do as Christians. We need to be open to the Lord and examine the evidence to see if our assumptions are correct. If, in fact, they are not, we have to trust that God can show us new, more effective ways to be His channels of salvation in the lost world to which He's sent us.

CHAPTER 3

THEY AREN'T
COMING IN

S o what's the problem with the church? For years I assumed it was
just my problem. Something was defective in me that caused me to
have trouble fitting in and getting along. Or maybe I just had a particularly bad run of luck in the churches I tried.

But in fact, national statistics on the church in America indicate my
personal experience with the church isn't at all uncommon. For the
majority of Americans, it may even be normative.

One fact that's quite clear about the lost in America today is that
very few of them are coming to church to look for answers. And yet,
don't most of us still believe that the way to reach others for Jesus is to
get them to come to church with us? Somehow, once they're there, the
programs or services or other people will eventually get them converted

and into the kingdom of God. We aren't at all sure how that's supposed to happen, but we do know for a fact that we have to get them to church first before anything else can happen. Right?

But what if we just can't get them to come to church?

MEET SOME OF MY FRIENDS

Allow me to introduce you to a few of my friends. Their perspectives and backgrounds are typical of many in their generation.

John and Sheila are two very good friends of mine. Sheila grew up in a nominal Catholic home where church attendance wasn't stressed. John's parents were active in a local Baptist church while his father was on his way up the ladder as a successful corporate executive. His father is now a top executive for a major Christian publishing firm.

John went to a well-known Christian college, where he graduated with top honors. He went on to Penn State University and earned a master's degree in counseling. There he met Sheila, who also shared his compassion for helping people and was enrolled in the same master's program. After they graduated they moved to our area to take jobs as counselors to court-adjudicated juvenile delinquents and their families.

Neither of them claims to be a Christian. After getting to know John, I asked him about this, and I was amazed at his explanation. He told me the primary reason he wasn't a Christian was because of the home he grew up in. "My parents are the two most manipulative and dishonest people I have ever known. In my entire extended family, many of whom are Christians, the only person who had any integrity at all was my grandfather—and he was a used car salesman!"

Phil and Kate Simons live in a bedroom suburb of Boston. Phil grew up in New Jersey, the son of a high-school teacher and coach. Kate grew up near Boston and summered in central New Hampshire. They met as college students at Boston University. After graduation they married and embarked on careers in the business world. Kate ended up as the vice president of sales for a large national rental car company before she quit work to have kids. Phil has an MBA and is on a fast track as a senior financial executive with a Fortune 50 consumer package goods firm. Now in their mid to late thirties, they have two young sons, a nice home in the suburbs, and a small farm in New Hampshire that they use as a vacation and weekend getaway. They've worked hard and are enjoying a measure of financial success. They live the "good life" and have happy, well-adjusted kids.

While both had nominal experiences with church as children (Phil was Catholic, Kate was Methodist), they don't look at the church as something they ought to consider. They have no idea why someone would want to put on uncomfortable clothes and go off to a strange building with strange music on a Sunday morning. What could the church offer them that they don't already have? Even if they were interested in church, Sunday is their family day, the only time they have for doing special activities with their kids in an altogether-too-busy week. They're outside the reach of the local church.

Lou and Cindy Page met and married in their midthirties. Like many in their generation, they had lived fairly fast and loose during their single-adult days. Now married with a young daughter, the Pages are looking for something of substance to help them build a lasting marriage and to be good parents. They've seen how the marriages of many of their friends are already breaking up.

Lou was raised in a nominally Protestant home, and Cindy's parents were committed Catholics. Both have a generalized belief in God but have no idea of how to connect relationally with Him.

They eventually decided to attend the local Catholic church where they were married. "Our hope," Lou told me, "was that we would get some spiritual direction and teaching for our lives from the services, and that we would get to meet other young parents who share an interest in spiritual growth. Each time we attend we feel terribly let down. The priest's sermons seem to have no bearing on life and are virtually the same each time. The parishioners tear out of the building after the service as if it's on fire. And we have yet to meet anyone, even though we've gone a half a dozen times in the past year."

Ted Breton was raised unchurched. He grew up, went to college, and landed a job in the television industry. He worked hard and rose quickly through the ranks. By the time he was thirty, he had a top job as a television producer in New York City, a beautiful house on Connecticut's Gold Coast, and a second home on a lake in the Catskills.

In his midthirties, he met Jesus and gave his life to Him. Ted found a local church and started to attend along with his family. He grew as a disciple, and God gave him a heart of concern for his lost friends in the world of television production. He knows his friends matter to God, and he cares deeply for them. But he felt that while his local church was a good place for his wife and kids, it wasn't the place to bring his secular friends from the business world. He knew, instinctively, that his local church was more likely to drive his friends away from God rather than draw them to Jesus.

WHAT THE RESEARCH SHOWS

Like Ted, many Christians today are experiencing frustration as they find more and more people in their lives who seem beyond the reach of the local church. This frustration is fairly widespread because the majority of Americans don't go to church and aren't interested or even open to going to church.

According to researcher George Barna, the number of Americans attending church on any given Sunday was only 49 percent in 1991. This figure declined rapidly to 37 percent in 1996 and has since edged slightly upward to 42 percent in 2001.[1] While we haven't succeeded in evangelizing our country, we've produced enough biological growth and modest levels of conversion growth that the church has held its own.

The younger the person, the more likely he or she is to be outside the influence of the church. For those in their late teens to midthirties, the weekly church attendance figure in 2000 was only 28 percent. That compares with 43 percent for those in their midthirties to midfifties, and 52 percent for those in their midfifties to midseventies.

The research also points out regional differences in church attendance figures. Here in the Northeast U.S., the average weekly church attendance is only 32 percent, compared to 37 percent in the West, 44 percent in the Midwest, and 46 percent in the South.

CULTURE GAP

People are staying away from church for a variety of reasons, some of which we have control over and some of which we do not.

We can describe many of these people as "culturally unchurched." They're simply not inclined to look to the church or to a pastor for help with spiritual issues or for information about God. This was very much my experience as a young person growing up in an unchurched household. It never occurred to me that people in the church had something that I might want.

Who are the culturally unchurched? Let's look at their opposites, those who are "culturally churched." These are people whose natural response to wanting to find out more about God or spiritual matters is to go to church or turn to a pastor. They may not actually be attending church, but they would feel comfortable going to church. The culturally unchurched, however, have significant cultural obstacles that keep them from even considering going to church. They're the same kind of feelings of discomfort that evangelical Christians might experience in considering whether to attend a worship service at a mosque, a synagogue, or a Buddhist temple. It's a scary thought! That's what a cultural barrier is.

The big picture of secular society's rejection of the church has to do with this growing culture gap. In a nation of exploding cultural diversification, ever-widening generational differences, and the rapid erosion of shared acceptance of the basic Judeo-Christian values upon which this country was built, the church has lost touch and become more and more marginalized. No longer is the gap between believers and nonbelievers just a spiritual one. The separation in cultural values between the church and non-Christians has widened over recent decades to become a huge chasm.

The problem isn't with the values of the people in the church. It's simply that those outside the church have had such an enormous shift in values. We're no longer in a culture that broadly shares our basic values and beliefs. We're in a culture of multiple layers of divergent and conflicting values that differ widely from those of the Bible. The cultural gap is now so great that we need a cross-cultural missions strategy to be able to effectively evangelize our own neighbors and coworkers and even family members for Christ.

The breach is especially gaping between young and old. The missions frontier today is no longer geographic—it's generational! Increasingly our distinctive values, attitudes, lifestyle, and worldview are predominantly defined and controlled by the particular generation into which we were born. The new mission fields are the lost and younger generations in our own country, in our own communities, perhaps even in our own homes.

It's clear that the younger generations have much less experience with the church and much less openness to it than those who are now in their midfifties and up who built the church as we know it today through their hard work, sacrificial giving, and faithful attendance. But without the younger generations, the church has no future.

Reinforcing the cultural barriers between churched and unchurched is the widespread perception of the church's lack of relevance. In one study, George Barna found that *even among those who regularly attend church,* more than half said that what goes on there is irrelevant to their daily lives.[2] So it shouldn't be surprising that most of those who stay away do not view church as relevant.

A recent Gallup poll asked, "If you were dying, to whom would you turn for spiritual guidance and comfort?" Only one-third of the adults in the United States said they would turn to a pastor or to a church, compared to 81 percent who would first turn to family members and 61 percent who said they would turn to friends.[3]

As a layperson involved in the business world as well as a consultant trained in church growth and missiology, I'm often asked to address groups of pastors on this issue of the church's relevance. I usually tell them to preach on the issues that people care about. For example, what do most men care about? The typical American husband and father, Christian or non-Christian, has three burning topics on his mind when he can't fall asleep at night: How can I survive in the workplace? How can I pass on my values to my kids? and How can I save my marriage? He's sweating bullets every day in an increasingly difficult, dishonest, and antagonistic marketplace. These are issues men care about, and if churches want to attract them, they need to share plainly what the Bible teaches on those particular issues.

Though I've shared this advice with thousands of pastors over the past decade, I see very few of them preaching messages on these kinds of meaningful issues.

BURNED

Many are culturally unchurched because they've had little or no experience with the church. Except for weddings and funerals, going to church simply hasn't been a part of their experience growing up or as an adult.

For others, their reason for not coming is not too little exposure to the church, but too much. Many have had a bad experience at church in the past. In *Exit Interviews: Revealing Stories of Why People Are Leaving the Church,* William D. Hendricks explores sixteen case studies that illustrate the frustration, heartache, and hurt of many who have bad experiences in the church that cause them to leave. For the most part, these people don't come back.

A few years ago I conducted a research study on this issue for the American Bible Society. Here are a few statements I heard from respondents about their bad experiences in church:

> I got divorced. When I got divorced, instead of support, they turned their backs on me.

> The pastor left the church, which put it in turmoil, with backbiting among members.

Two of my children were made fun of in church. They were putting down other people, then putting down other religions.

My father was dying in the hospital, and I asked the pastor to visit, but he never returned phone calls or made a visit.

Our membership split and it created a lot of ill will.

Two pastors were fighting for power, and deacons supporting the pastors pulled guns out in the church.

The priest's homilies put down teenagers; I was a teenager at the time.

The preacher wanted everyone to chip in to buy his son a Cadillac.

Because I went to public high school, the priest told me I would never get the kind of education I needed.

The deacons didn't approve of us living together before we were married.

I got counseling for domestic abuse—they wanted me to go back to my ex-husband.

The pastor was a crook.

The minister came to see me in the hospital and told me I was there because I hadn't been to church.

Pastor was arrested...it had something to do with money. [4]

Too often, and in too many ways, the church has been its own worst enemy when it comes to reaching those outside its walls.

CHAPTER 4

GIVING CHURCH A TRY

L et me take you back to that day I left Moffit's house and knelt on
the sidewalk to give my life to God. I knew I'd been lost and that
now I was found by Jesus. And I knew I could talk to God by praying.
But that was it. I didn't know how to begin growing because I had no
idea how my new experience connected with anything else in God's
plan.

I thought the Bible was for people who had gone off on some kind
of intellectual head trip. Church, I assumed, was some deviant form of
faith that had veered off the track from God centuries ago. I supposed
it was people's way of filling the vacuum when they didn't have a relationship with God through Jesus Christ. One day on a train I spotted
a clergyman (his black shirt with the funny white collar was a dead

giveaway). I smiled and said, "Peace, man, Jesus loves you." If looks could kill, his expression would have toasted me. So I didn't regard pastors as people who could give me advice about growing with Jesus.

FRIENDS

For that first year of my faith, it was just Jesus and me—walking and praying through life together. I had no help from anyone else. I just had to do the best I could and try to survive. It wasn't pretty, but I not only survived, I started to grow.

For the remainder of the summer I continued living under the boardwalk in Ocean City. My lifestyle afforded me the opportunity to meet and befriend many people my own age. I often used a book of Rod McKuen poems as a springboard to get into conversations about God. Not a very orthodox approach, but over the next month or so I led a half-dozen young people to Jesus.

The following summer, I returned to Ocean City and ran into one of those young converts. She told me about meeting a guy who gave her a Bible. Later, she introduced me to him—a seminary student running a coffeehouse outreach. He gave me a paperback copy of the *Good News* New Testament and told me these were letters from God for followers of Jesus. So I started reading them and connecting with God in a new dimension.

I read this exciting stuff about Jesus and the disciples and the apostle Paul and first-century Christians. Now what I wanted to know was how to lead the same kind of radically obedient life here in the

USA in the late 1960s. I desperately wanted to grow with God, to walk in the Spirit, and to connect with other followers of Jesus.

In high school that fall, a fellow in my senior English class invited me to a meeting called a Young Life Club. He picked me up, and we went to a house where about forty-five kids were gathered, most of them from my school's jock and cheerleader social set. At the time I was pretty firmly into the hippie clique—wearing my genuine army surplus field coat, having just returned from Woodstock, and often skipping school to attend antiwar rallies. But I didn't care what social group anyone else came from. I was delighted to find others who knew Jesus and wanted to follow Him.

From my very first meeting, I was excited about the Young Life group's culturally relevant form and its focus on Jesus. I wanted all my friends to come and meet Jesus too, and I started to invite them to join us. Within six weeks well over a hundred kids were coming to club each week. About 20 percent were from the original jock and cheerleader set. The rest were my friends—with beads, long hair, torn and patched bell-bottom jeans, denim vests, and marginal reputations. I can hardly blame the many original members of the club who left after being sur-rounded by this motley crew. Yet in spite of their outward appearance of rebellion, a lot of these marginalized kids were seeking a higher authority in life. Many of these seekers of truth and freedom found both in the person of Jesus Christ before the year was out.

I also loved the adult leaders in the Young Life Club. Two of the men opened their lives to me and started to invest in me and disciple me. Their mentoring poured the fuel on my fire to know God and walk with Him each day. I was smart enough to know I needed such living, in-the-flesh role models to help me learn how to walk with Jesus in the modern world. For the next four years I really grew as I was discipled, and I served as a volunteer leader in the Young Life ministry in my hometown and at college.

CONNECTING WITH CHURCH

As a growing believer, I knew there was supposed to be some kind of connection between being a Christian and going to church. But I just couldn't figure out what it was.

While I was still in high school, I went with a group of Young Life friends to a small church. There were probably less than a hundred people there. I expected it to be warm and friendly. We went in and mingled before the service started, but no one spoke to us. We sat through the service. Afterward people around us greeted and chatted with those they knew and then left. No one ever spoke to us. Weird. Bizarre. It was all ceremony and no relationships. Even funerals had more interaction between people than this church service had.

When I was nineteen and in college, several Young Life friends and I decided to run a Christian coffeehouse as a summer outreach ministry. A local Methodist church let us use their old church building, which was next door to their new sanctuary. We met with the pastor, a gracious and caring man who had a heart for the lost and unchurched youth in the neighborhood but had little understanding of how we wanted to reach them. He told us we could use the old church building because it had been officially "desanctified," whatever that meant.

Each night before we opened the coffeehouse, the other staff members and I would gather for Bible study and prayer. One night the pastor dropped by to say hello, and I invited him to join us in our prayer time. I had previously decided to conclude this prayer time with communion—using Kool-Aid and Oreos. When I pulled out the drink and cookies and announced what we were going to do, the pastor's face turned white. Not knowing then what I know now, I was a little surprised when he excused himself and left. I figured he just had more pressing church business elsewhere.

Later I spent a summer on the Jersey shore working in a coffeehouse ministry to the teens who wandered the boardwalk and the streets. One Sunday I went to the church that sponsored this ministry, and afterward the senior pastor offered to invest some time mentoring me. This was what I'd been looking for. Unfortunately, when I showed up for my appointment later in the week, the pastor made a pass at me. He was a homosexual and used "discipleship meetings" in his church office to try to seduce young men. That encounter set me back for a while in accepting church.

I finally connected again with church in my early twenties when a friend took me to Park Street Church in Boston. Talk about culture shock! Behind a pulpit that towered at least sixteen feet from the floor stood pastors wearing flowing black robes that made them look like specters from…well, from hell. The music clearly wasn't Newport Folk Festival—the soloists were opera singers who might have been singing in Italian or in English; I couldn't tell. The congregation chanted creeds, prayers, and weird stuff that everyone but me seemed to know by heart. I mumbled along quietly and tried to hide my embarrassment.

But unlike my previous church exposures, at Park Street I found a group of committed friends. I think that's what saved me. I'll be eternally grateful for these guys who invested so much in my spiritual growth. During the week, we had Bible study together, prayed for people on our college campus, and spent a lot of time together hanging out and having fun. There was just this one weird thing they always wanted to do: church on Sunday.

Eventually I adjusted to it. And it was there, in the Park Street Church balcony, that I met and wooed Martie, the wonderful woman who has been my wife for the past twenty-five years. So I can hardly say I never got anything out of church! The truth is, from all my time in that historic church on the Boston Common, I received a great deal of training and ministry experience, plus many lifelong friends.

EXCITING OUTREACH

As I was getting somewhat acclimated to the church through my friends at Park Street, I found that many others in the church's college ministry shared the same burden my friends and I had for reaching out to lost people. And they were doing something about it.

I joined them by getting involved in campus ministry at MIT in Cambridge. It was exciting. Almost every week, somewhere in the small group of graduate students I was working with, we would see lost people found. One guy was a graduate student from South Africa. Another was a U.S. Army captain home on leave. Another was a top salesman for Digital Equipment Corporation in Europe who later married a young woman from Park Street Church, and they've served as missionaries to businesspeople in Europe for the past two decades.

I also spent a summer working with students at Northeastern University in Boston. Again, it was incredible to see God work in people's lives. Nick was a six-foot-four, strapping, powerful man's man from Pawtucket, Rhode Island. He rowed varsity on Northeastern's heavyweight eight-man crew team. The year before I met him, Nick's team went to England and won the Henley on the Thames, the most prestigious race in the world of sculling. Nick had a Christian friend from high school who challenged him to consider the claims of Christ. At one point, this friend told Nick the story of Gideon and the fleece. Nick decided to test God and see if this Jesus he was hearing about was really the way to God. One night he prayed, "Lord, if you are real and you are Jesus, when I go down to my car in the morning, would you have the ashtray full of water?"

The next morning Nick got up. The sky was clear. He went downstairs and got in his beat-up '62 Chevy Impala and found the ashtray full of water. Nick was convinced. He prayed and accepted Christ as his Savior on the spot.

Nick began to grow in Christ, and together we started to pray for his roommates at college and his friends on the crew team. Within a couple years most of his roommates and many of his crew friends had become believers. Today these people are still in touch and form a powerful network of committed believers spanning the globe. It all started with a wet ashtray in an old Chevy.

MY VISION

I graduated from Gordon College with a degree in biblical and theological studies, then married Martie. As a student of the Bible, I recognized the pivotal role the church plays in God's plans for mankind and the world. At the same time, I continued to find my church experience quite difficult. As I got more and more involved in the local church, I had a hard time finding people there who shared my compassion for the lost souls outside the church.

Meanwhile I quit my job and went to Fuller Seminary in Pasadena, California, to study church growth and missiology with Donald McGavran and Peter Wagner. I honestly thought if I knew more of the "right stuff," I could help my own church and other churches begin to reach out to lost people.

My time at Fuller was exciting. I was hanging out with people who had a tremendous heart for reaching lost people, and I was being taught and mentored by leaders who knew how to find lost people and had actually done it.

While most other church growth practitioners worked with large denominations (like the Southern Baptists, who were planting 500 new churches a year), I had a different vision. God convinced me to pray for and focus on the 350,000 existing churches in America. He gave me a vision of myself as the country doctor to these congregations, making the rounds like the doctor in his buggy a century ago. There might not be much money in this calling, I told myself, but think of the kingdom good that could come from it! Each of those congregations averaged a hundred people, and if over the course of ten years each church could add just a hundred new people, why, the number of believers in America could be doubled! Thirty-five million new believers from existing churches alone! Just think how many lost people could be found during the course of our lifetime!

It was a great vision and a God-sized goal, but it didn't match my subsequent experience.

WHY CAN'T WE DO MORE?

Over the years I've attended and been part of many different kinds of churches—independent, evangelical, conservative mainline, liberal mainline, fundamentalist, separatistic, and more. I've been involved with some of the most famous megachurches of our day. I've been part of churches where not only did the ministers wear robes, but the ushers wore tuxedos. In California I went to churches where men wore lemon-colored leisure suits. In other churches people sang in tongues, were "slain in the Spirit," and were more likely to bring a tambourine to the service than a Bible.

In the Appalachian foothills of north Georgia, I attended a snake-handling church. The people sang, danced, pranced, and finally opened the snake box on the altar and started pulling out what looked to be fully functioning and wide-awake timber rattlers, copperheads, and cane rattlers. They continued dancing, singing, and praying while holding as many as five snakes at a time. Then they would pass on the snakes to other worshipers. I sat close to the back, right next to the door. Whew! That was a church service where people paid attention!

Some of the churches we've been part of over the years were large, and some were small. One United Methodist Church we were part of was so small my daughter Megan, who was three or four at the time, had a Sunday school class all her own. Her teacher, a dear woman, showed up faithfully every week with a well-prepared lesson and taught her heart out as if she had a class of fifty excited preschoolers.

For a number of years we were involved in a large Presbyterian church in an eastern city. This church focused on the executive set in our community—well-educated, white-collar executives and professionals. No other church in our area was effectively reaching this particular socioeconomic group with the gospel. The sanctuary seated about 750, and we had about 1,100 in two services on Sunday mornings. While the church wasn't operating anywhere near capacity, we had well over 2,000 adult visitors annually. Of those, less than 200 were added to membership each year. After losses from people dying, moving, or leaving, the annual net gain might be 10 or 20 people at best. The doors were wide open, lots of people came to visit, and many of them stayed for a while, but a very high proportion never got enfolded into the body.

The membership process was quite drawn out and cumbersome. On average it took well over six months of various steps to join the church. Having become good friends with many on the pastoral staff, I finally raised the question at lunch with them one day: "Why can't we do more to reach out to and enfold the thousands of people who visit the church each year?"

The senior pastor answered, "Bruce, it's like a fine restaurant. If you have a successful restaurant and lots of people want to get in, you don't go and double your seating. You make people wait in line. The ones who really want to get in will wait long enough until they finally are seated. The rest can go eat somewhere else. That's the way I see it with our church."

I asked where else in our city these people could go where they could hear the gospel with their own kind of people. The response was painful silence.

It was a response that mirrored the predominant attitude I've seen in almost every church. As I continued to be involved in a number of different churches, it was hard to find people who were interested in combing the woods, finding the lost, and bringing them into the family of God. For the most part other church members seemed caught up with their own marriages and families, their work, and perhaps a few friends from church. Most evaluated their church in terms of meeting personal needs and the needs of their families, while giving little thought to the spiritually lost who surrounded them. In response to this expectation, the ministries and programs of the church were primarily directed at meeting the needs of those who were already part of the church family.

Even in churches that had strong evangelical ties and strongly stated commitments to evangelism, we actually saw and experienced very little evangelism for the most part. Most churches seemed to have a largely inward focus. Their priorities and commitments usually provided a lot of services for those already in the church. Even if there had been a genuine interest in going out to reach lost people, most members were so busy in their involvement with the church's major programs that they simply had no time left for outsiders.

CHAPTER 5

STILL SEARCHING

I used to get into heated debates with my best friend Dave Morgan, who was the founding pastor of the church Martie and I had helped start near Princeton. From passages like Matthew 28:18-19 and Colossians 1:28, I argued that the church's primary purpose was to reach lost people, lead them to Christ, and help them grow to maturity in Him.

"No," Dave would say, basing his answer on his training at a well-known evangelical seminary. "The primary purpose of the church is to nurture those who are in it. Our job as church leaders is to equip the saints for the work of ministry."

But I couldn't agree with him.

STARTING AFRESH

There were times when I was hopeful. At one point Martie and I helped plant a new church near Princeton, New Jersey. It was very exciting. The church started with eight families. Of course, everyone was committed to growth. It was the only way we would survive! Week after week our core group showed up with new people in tow. Some of them were actually non-Christians who made a commitment to Christ and started to grow.

This positive trend kept up until our Sunday attendance reached about 125 or 150. Then came a subtle change. Instead of an eager "Look, there's someone new!" the attitude among some of the regulars shifted to, "Who are all these new people anyway? They're getting in the way of time with my friends!"

When we bought an old turkey farm and restored the barn into a church building, we experienced a renaissance of the original welcoming attitude toward new people. We wanted all the new people we could get. We needed their help to pay for the building!

But by the time Sunday attendance passed three hundred, our conversion evangelism trailed off. Most newcomers were already Christians when they showed up and were changing churches because they liked what we had to offer. Our church was growing, but the kingdom of God was not. We really weren't doing anything to seek out the lost people who made up the vast majority of those who lived around us.

IN THE CORPORATE WORLD

After I'd finished my studies at Fuller Seminary, I embarked on a career in the corporate world. For the next twenty years I held a variety of positions in marketing research, marketing, and strategic planning. Much of my work was conducted in the consumer package goods field. My workday was taken up with M&M/Mars, Johnson & Johnson, Crayola Crayons, Campbell Soup, and other well-known firms selling products to consumers.

My involvement in the business world allowed me to build friendships with many non-Christians. Some of them were quite open to spiritual issues and to God Himself. But how could I take them to my church to learn more about God? Most churches seem to be blind, deaf, and dumb to the needs of any newcomer, let alone newcomers who may not be committed believers.

Over the years I've found that churches holding the same theological beliefs I do are not usually good places to take seekers. They tend to want to run a doctrinal purity test on every new person who walks through the door. This approach usually doesn't work too well for a person who has no doctrine at all but is only curious to learn about Jesus.

By default, I end up taking my friends to churches that are much more theologically liberal than I am. At least these churches tend to be more tolerant and accepting of new people. The downside is that often the gospel preached there is so vague and confusing it doesn't provide much help to seekers.

Sometimes I had a small group I could invite non-Christians to. Often I was left trying to minister on my own, with the help of my family or a few mature Christian friends. But church was just not a safe or helpful environment when it came to reaching out to lost people.

CHURCH CONSULTANT

As I continued my career in marketing, I always found time on the side to work as a consultant to churches, denominations, and parachurch ministries. This work never paid the bills, but it was my first love. I really wanted to help those who wanted to reach out and enfold lost people.

Much of what I learned in my jobs in market research and marketing dovetailed nicely with what I'd learned from courses in missiology and church growth. Together these skills enabled me to help those who wanted to reach the lost, or at least attract more people to their particular church or ministry.

Churches often looked for consulting help when they had a clearly defined problem. Usually they had a desire to grow, but various obstacles kept them from moving forward. The church growth perspectives and some of the tools in my tool kit helped many of these churches begin to grow.

As I gained experience and had "successful" assignments in churches that I could go back and visit, I began to see a pattern emerge. Yes, we'd overcome serious obstacles to growth. We had better services, new ministries, bigger parking lots, and streamlined organizations. Churches were doing a better job at meeting people's needs and a better job at marketing their ministries. The result was increased growth in that particular congregation. But most of the growth seemed to come from transfers from other churches—people who were already Christians. It was hard to find much evidence of conversion growth taking place. The kingdom of God wasn't really growing. People weren't being moved from the camp of the lost into God's forever family.

After twenty years as an advocate of church growth philosophies and strategies, I began to have gnawing doubts about the value of any of these efforts in God's eternal economy.

A NEW ENGLAND STRATEGY

My desire to reach out and help find lost people continued unabated. Working in the business world and having some solid relationships with non-Christians in my neighborhood convinced me the need was great. So many of these people were really open to spiritual issues and to God. My frustration was to figure out a workable strategy to connect them to Jesus.

In 1981 I was hired by a large regional evangelism ministry in New England to help them develop a strategic plan. The plan was designed to help their two thousand constituent churches begin to do conversion evangelism and reach unchurched people in the six-state region. The final plan was widely applauded and supported by the leadership, the staff, and the board of this ministry.

But the plan was never implemented. The churches continued plowing ahead with business as usual. The need was great and the strategy was sound. But finding people willing to put the needs of lost people ahead of their own inward-focused agendas seemed extraordinarily hard to do.

As life went on, God kept bringing my thoughts back to that strategy for New England. He kept telling me that if someone would pick up that strategy and implement it, many lost people could be reached for Christ in my lifetime.

The strategy was really quite simple. To help churches grow through conversion evangelism, the first step was to support, encourage, and equip pastors—the key to any church's growth and success. The pastor's vision and priorities pretty much determine what can be done by a congregation. But pastors and their families are under tremendous pressure today. Most are poorly equipped, even after seminary, to lead a church. On average, more than half of all pastors quit the ministry within ten years of leaving seminary, and less than one in ten will complete an entire career in the ministry. In New England the average pastor stays only three years in a church before moving on, even though research indicates that it takes at least five to seven years at a church before a pastor attains effectiveness in his leadership there. So supporting and nurturing pastoral leadership was our strategy's first goal.

The second leg of our New England plan was to train lay leaders in church leadership, church growth, and evangelism. A pastor can't lead a church alone; he needs a strong team of lay leaders who are knowledgeable on the issues and are trained in the appropriate skills.

The final step was to put together a regional pool of shared resources to help churches with evangelism and church growth. Many of these tools and services are expensive and difficult to provide on the budget of the typical local congregation. A pool of shared expertise would allow thousands of churches access to needed support at a very low cost per church.

TEAMING UP

Several years after this strategy was developed, I was on a business trip and stopped in to visit my pastor friend Dave Morgan in Princeton. God had called Dave and me to minister side by side in quite a few situations since our student days together on the campus of Gordon College. As we talked, Dave shared a vision God had given him while on vacation on Squam Lake in New Hampshire the previous summer. It was then that Dave and I realized how much we shared a mutual burden to help support church leaders and start a new wave of evangelism and church growth efforts.

As I flew back home to Chicago at the end of that trip, God impressed on me that He really wanted to do something about this. If other Christian leaders in New England didn't want to pursue a strategy to help churches grow through conversion evangelism, could He possibly be calling Dave and me to do something about it?

What followed were four years of research, prayer, networking, exploration, and more prayer. This preparation culminated in December of 1986 when Dave resigned his position as senior pastor after ten years at his church and moved his family to Wolfeboro, New Hampshire, to help establish what we named The Leadership Center. Backed by an independent board of key evangelical leaders and a small but highly committed group of financial supporters, Dave set about taking a leadership role in helping make our God-given vision for New England a reality.

Over the next couple of years, my primary role in this fledgling ministry was as a financial supporter and active board member. I made frequent trips to New Hampshire for board meetings or just to encourage Dave and his family. I continued to be impressed by the spiritual need and the potential for church growth in New England.

A DIFFERENT CALLING

Gradually the conviction grew within Martie and me that God was leading me to quit my business career to move to New England to become a catalyst for evangelism and church growth there.

In the spring of 1988, I resigned from my marketing position with M&M/Mars. Martie and I and our eight- and six-year-old daughters moved to a small town on the shores of Lake Winnipesaukee in central New Hampshire. The culture shock in moving from the life of a big-city, fast-track, corporate executive to that of a "missionary" in a New Hampshire town of less than five thousand was intense. God, as always, proved faithful. He helped us adjust to all the changes, and, after a couple of years, we were almost "normal" again.

During my first year in this ministry, God gave me a significant promise. He led me to the passage in Genesis 12 where God said to Abram,

> Leave your country, your people and your father's house-
> hold and go to the land I will show you. I will make you
> into a great nation and I will bless you; I will make your
> name great, and you will be a blessing. I will bless those

who bless you, and whoever curses you I will curse; and all peoples on earth will be blessed through you. (verses 1-3)

God encouraged me to look at how He'd abundantly fulfilled these promises for Abraham. He also encouraged me to remember, whenever I felt regret for all I'd left behind, that He was calling me to a special ministry. He would help me through the tough times and provide what my family and I needed.

God also made it plain that there was still a "promised land" where He wanted to lead me and other believers, a land "flowing with milk and honey." What He showed me is that the promised land today is people—the lives of all who are lost in this world and without hope in the next. These are the people God intends to lead us to. He'll allow us to be part of the process as He captures and reclaims these lost children for His eternal family.

Finally, from this passage God gave me a real conviction that He would bless my life by letting me play a key role in helping to reach many lost people for Jesus.

CHAPTER 6

WE AREN'T
GOING OUT

——————

Thirteen-year-old Brian Robeson was a passenger in a single-engine plane flying over the Canadian wilderness when the pilot suffered a fatal heart attack, and the plane went down. Brian survived the crash but found himself alone in the wilderness with nothing but the clothes on his back and a hatchet his mother had given him as a present. His story is told in *Hatchet*, by Gary Paulsen.

Recovering from the shock of the crash, Brian took heart as he concluded with certainty that he would be the object of an intensive search.

> They would look for him. For the plane. His father and
> mother would be frantic. They would tear the world apart
> to find him. Brian had seen searches on the news, seen

movies about lost planes. When a plane went down, they mounted extensive searches and almost always found the plane within a day or two. Pilots all filed flight plans—a detailed plan for where and when they were going to fly. They would come; they would look for him. The searchers would get government planes and cover both sides of the flight plan filed by the pilot and search until they found him.[5]

What Brian didn't know was that the plane had veered significantly off course before finally crashing. As a result, the initial search effort turned up nothing and was abandoned after two weeks. Brian had to endure an incredible ordeal lasting fifty-four days until he finally was rescued. But his hope and belief that eventually someone would come sustained him through the most difficult of circumstances.

Is there hope for the hundreds of millions who are spiritually lost in America today? Can they realistically expect to be intensively searched for by those who alone are able to rescue them—those who would "tear the world apart" to find the lost? Very few non-Christians will get lucky and stumble out of the woods on their own. Very few will accidentally bump into someone on the edge of the woods, as I did, who will help them find a way out and a way to God.

Committed Christians are the primary instruments God uses to find lost people in our world. The local church, the people of God, are His first and foremost rescue squad. But these lost Americans are not going to get found while we spend the biggest part of our Christian lives inside the church building worshiping God. They aren't going to be found while the church stays inside its holy huddle and prays for the lost. We must go where they are and find them.

IN TROUBLE

This principle of incarnational theology is clearly evidenced in Scripture and demonstrated throughout all of recorded history as God's chosen strategy to reach and redeem lost people. This is particularly true of the call to evangelism and discipleship that we see in the Gospels and in the book of Acts. God's command is that we go out where the lost are to search and work diligently that some may be found and brought into God's forever family.

Yet now, at the beginning of the twenty-first century, most churches are operating on a different philosophy. Their basic assumption is that the lost are expected to turn up in church on Sunday morning to hear about the love of Jesus and get connected into a saving relationship with God. Those few Christians who think much about how to reach the lost focus most often on how to make church services more attractive to seekers.

But this strategy is at best a forlorn hope. The local church as we know it is not reaching our nation for Christ. Not only has the church lost the ability to go outside itself to reach and redeem the millions of lost people in America, it's even losing the ability to maintain and reproduce itself.

"Wait," you may say, "do you mean—the church is in trouble?

Didn't Jesus say, 'I will build my church; and the gates of hell shall not prevail against it'?"

You're right. That's what Jesus said—in Matthew 16:18 (KJV). To understand what those words mean, however, we need to be clear that they refer to the people of God gathered under the leadership of Christ, and not to any particular local congregation or any particular form of organizational structure. The Holy Roman Empire—a dominant political and religious structure of the Middle Ages that combined government and church—no longer exists, but that doesn't mean the church of Christ has been diminished. Instead, the church has grown and multiplied in new forms.

When Western missionaries were tossed out of China and the churches closed when Communism triumphed there in 1950, there were only a few hundred thousand Christians. In succeeding decades, while the church form appeared to have been extinguished, it was actually alive and growing in new forms—the house church movement. Today the number of Chinese Christians is estimated at more than fifty million.

The fact is, the church in today's world is predominantly alive, healthy, and growing. Leading global church researchers report Bible believing Christians are multiplying at a rate three times faster than world population growth. In Asia, Latin America, and Africa, the Christian church is exploding.

That's the good news. The bad news is that the church in the West, especially in America, is not doing well. It's not so much the cause of Christ that's in trouble but the particular form we've followed here in the West for the past few hundred years.

SPIRITUALLY STERILE

Here are some facts from various sources that highlight the problem. Eighty percent of the churches in America are stagnant or declining. Between 3,500 and 4,000 local congregations (over 10 percent of all churches in America) close their doors each year. Fewer than 10 percent of churches in America regularly see conversion evangelism taking place in their ministries.

While megachurches have been the big news on the American church scene for the last two decades, research has found that 80 percent of their increase is transfer growth—not from conversions, but from Christians moving from smaller churches to larger ones.

Meanwhile, perhaps as many as nine of every ten born-again Christians are spiritually sterile—genuinely converted, yet never growing to the point of being able to share their faith with another person, let alone help someone meet Jesus, or begin to grow as a disciple.

Think what would happen if nine of every ten women of child-bearing age in the United States were suddenly unable to reproduce and bear healthy children. In short order we would see a tremendous decline in our birth rate and eventually in our population. This is essentially what's happening with the church on a spiritual level. Our congregations are full of infants and children who never grow up. The maturity and multiplication of disciples are rare. Moreover, of the Christian outreach that does occur, most of it is actually *evangelism inside the church,* largely among believers' children, particularly preteens.

A MORE RESISTANT WORLD?

Many of my friends in the church believe that our problem is not that the church is losing its effectiveness but that people in our post-Christian, postmodern secular culture are so much more resistant to the gospel than people were in the past. But is that really the case?

Here in New England, church leaders often bemoan the "fact" that the population of our six-state region is so increasingly hardened and resistant to spiritual matters and the gospel. Such perceptions about the spiritual barrenness here are widespread and firmly held. But the success of the Mormons disproves this point of view.

The Church of Jesus Christ of Latter-day Saints—better known as the Mormon Church—is the fastest-growing church in the world, with a growth rate internationally of 45 percent in the past decade. What's especially disconcerting to my fellow New Englanders is that over the last decade the Mormons have had a faster growth rate in New England than they have had worldwide—58 percent in the six states of this region. This explosive growth has led the Mormons to construct their first temple in New England in the Boston suburb of Belmont.

Why is this religious group growing so rapidly? Most likely it can be attributed to the fact that the Mormons are heavily committed to and involved in evangelism. The Mormons see high levels of conversion evangelism simply because they're *doing* evangelism, and doing it outside their church.

Many, many non-Christians today are searching for spiritual direction. Many people are open to and interested in learning more about God. The church's problem in the United States is not the unresponsiveness of the population but rather *our refusal to get involved in reaching lost people.* In essence the church has gotten lost itself and has forgotten what God has kept us here to do. For centuries we were winning the world to Christ; now we're not only failing to do evangelism outside the church, we're failing increasingly to reach our own children.

MYTHS WE CLING TO

In recent years George Barna has been warning church leaders across the nation about what he calls the ten myths of evangelism. With extensive research he exposes the lack of supporting evidence for our perceptions that churches are committed to evangelism, or that they're effectively preparing people for evangelism, or that most Christians are actively involved in evangelism and doing it well. He notes survey results revealing that less than half of our pastors include evangelism in their church's top three priorities, that only one of every three Christians believes they have a responsibility to share their faith, and that only one out of five prays consistently for the salvation of others.

I would add another myth to Barna's list—what I call the myth of trickle-down evangelism. Conventional wisdom holds that if you simply do a good job feeding the Christians within the local church—through quality worship, teaching, and fellowship—then somehow evangelism will "trickle down" through the congregation and out into the world. (I even heard a Christian leader say once that all a church needs to have healthy growth is good worship, good fellowship, and okay management.) This trickle-down philosophy is shared by thousands of church and denominational leaders and is taught in many seminaries in America.

But it isn't true. It's a powerful myth that we *want* to believe, but the "trickle" simply isn't happening. If, because of our blindness, we continue to hold to our belief in such myths, it could cause the church enormous harm in the future.

God is going to have to intervene to change our patterns and paradigms so that we can break out of this backwater and become all that He means us to be.

FIGHTING GRAVITY

Our approach to evangelism reminds me of a bumper sticker I once saw that said, "FIGHT GRAVITY." When I told my wife I just had to get one for my car, Martie said, "Are you nuts? You can't fight gravity. Everybody knows that."

That's the reaction most people have to that phrase. Fight gravity? That's dumb! It can't be done! But think about it: Of course you can fight gravity. We do it every day. We ride in an elevator or take an escalator. We fly in an airplane. Some people have even gone to the moon and back. We fight gravity all the time—and win! To do so requires only a correct understanding of how to overcome it. After that, it's so easy it becomes commonplace.

When we're really honest, most of us say, "Well, I know I'm supposed to do evangelism and be a witness for Christ, but I've tried it and it never worked for me." In *Today's Pastors,* Barna writes,

> Most unfortunate is how lay evangelists often feel after their first attempt to share their faith. In research we conducted several years ago, those people told us that they generally emerge from their evangelistic adventure not with a feeling of joy, obedience, impact, hope, or gratitude, but with a *feeling of defeat.* Not recognizing that the job of converting people from a sinful to a forgiven state is the task of the Holy Spirit, most lay evangelists assume that the lack of evidence of a changed life means they have failed God, the church, the unconverted person, and themselves. Consequently, Christians appear to be sharing their faith less often than in the past.[6]

That reminds me of my early attempts at flying as a kid when, in Superman fashion, I tied an old sheet around my neck and jumped off my dad's cinderblock pile. Ouch! Boy, did that hurt.

Later I strapped an eight-inch plank—"wings"—across the handlebars of my bicycle. I pedaled as fast as I could down the steepest hill in our neighborhood. I figured that with enough speed I could achieve liftoff. Instead, I lost control and crashed.

I finally concluded that these approaches simply weren't workable. Fortunately, I didn't conclude that I'd never be able to fly. God in His grace has allowed me the chance to leave earth in many kinds of aircraft.

There's still nothing I enjoy more than taking off from a lake in a bush plane to head north to new adventures in the wilderness. I'm glad I didn't give up just because of a few setbacks early in my career of fighting gravity. I'd have missed out on so many wonderful experiences that God created me to enjoy.

It's the same way with sharing our faith. Many of us have a friend who regularly shares with strangers on airplanes and has people praying to receive Jesus. But when we try it…well, it's a lot like me diving off the cinderblock pile. We feel tongue-tied, fearful, embarrassed, rejected, or just plain awkward. Often the relationship never recovers from our well-meaning attempts. To so many of us, the whole notion of evangelism and witnessing eventually seems so wildly undoable that it causes us real discomfort, and even guilt and fear, to even consider it.

But it's a lot more doable than most of us imagine. It may be that what you tried wasn't really God's strategy for sharing your faith but rather some false notion many of us have picked up about what evangelism is and how it's done.

WHAT'S THE RIGHT STRATEGY?

So what *is* God's strategy for our effective evangelism today?

Is it simply inviting people to come hear an evangelistic speaker?

Before the advent of radio and motion pictures in the early twentieth century, one of the most common and popular forms of informing and entertaining people was through public lectures. Mark Twain earned his living primarily giving lectures in the late 1800s. Winston

Churchill did the same in the early 1900s. So for the church to use the same approach—a speaker in a building standing before an audience—was a culturally relevant strategy. But when was the last time you and your friends attended a public lecture? Most of us simply don't get information or entertainment that way anymore. In fact, for those of us who attend a traditional church with a traditional sermon, that's probably the only event in our lives that's driven by that old-time lecture format. It's the exception, not the rule.

Could our best evangelism strategy be another door-to-door program or approaching people in the mall?

Imagine a young single man asking your advice about finding a wife. You would answer, "Go to the mall and look around until you find an attractive girl of the right age. Then approach her and ask, 'Are you married?' If she replies, 'No,' then ask, 'Will you marry me?'" Right? Wrong. But that's essentially what we do in a lot of evangelism.

Or could our best strategy simply be to get our church to adopt whatever it is that all the big successful churches are doing to attract people?

My friend Don, a church consultant, took a trip to southern California to visit twenty megachurches. Each has a strong, growing ministry. Don asked the leaders of each church, "What's the key to your growth?" Don reported later, "They gave me twenty different answers! They said, 'It's prayer, it's small groups, it's drama, it's biblical preaching, it's family life, it's neighborhood services, it's VBS....'" His experience illustrates the futility of trying to transfer programs from one church to another.

So what *is* God's evangelism strategy for us?

Gifts and Calling

First, let me clarify a point that confuses many believers. God doesn't call all believers to be *evangelists.* Evangelism is a spiritual gift. There's a big difference between the spiritual gift of evangelism and simply sharing your faith. Billy Graham has the spiritual gift of evangelism. When he shares, people come forward by the hundreds and thousands. But have you listened to his messages? Pretty simple stuff. I suppose Billy Graham could get up and read from the phone book and people would still stream forward and accept Christ. It isn't his sermon; it's the Holy Spirit at work through his spiritual gift.

Most of us don't have the gift of evangelism. Researchers say only about one in ten Christians has it. If you have it, you've already seen some fruit in sharing your faith. That's great. I encourage you to cultivate your gift and use it.

While most of us are not called to a gifted ministry of evangelism, *all believers are called to be witnesses for Christ.* This is a role every Christian is to learn how to live out. Scripture is clear on this. For example, in 1 Peter 3:15 we're told, "Always be prepared to give an answer to everyone who asks you to give the reason for the hope that you have."

We're all called to be witnesses for Jesus. But being a witness isn't the same thing as doing evangelism. "Witness" is actually a legal term. A witness can share only within tight parameters: You can't give second-hand testimony. You can't give hearsay evidence. You can share only your own personal experience.

While evangelism is a gift God uses to reach people in special circumstances—especially those who have no contact at all with followers of Jesus—witnessing is the method God uses to reach people in an everyday way, especially those who have some relational contact with Christians. That includes the people we work with, socialize with, live near, and are related to. Witnessing is particularly effective with people who have such things in common with us.

THE POWER OF RELATIONSHIPS

This is exactly the approach God Himself used to bring us back into relationship with Him. Look at the Bible. He tried the cognitive knowledge approach through the Law and the Prophets. Guess what? We didn't get it. So He sent His Son to live among us, to hang out with us, to model God's love in a personal way. That's the essence of witnessing (as contrasted with evangelizing). It's the Jesus Plan—the strategy Jesus used, and the strategy He intends for us to use.

When a believer is in deliberate, frequent, genuinely motivated contact with non-Christians and has the basic skills to build relationships, trust will develop in such relationships to the point of openness. Open non-Christians can then have the gospel explained in a clear and relevant way and have the opportunity to respond to the claims of Christ. If the believer also has basic skills in helping the new believer get started on the road of discipleship, the process can be completed.

Relationships are the most powerful way in which people today are reached and changed. Approaches that don't reflect this truth simply don't work well anymore.

Relationally driven witnessing means praying about the potential for a relationship, taking steps to get to know the other person, having common experiences together, talking together, and learning to communicate and develop increasing levels of trust. As the relationship develops, as communication and trust grow deeper—then share. It takes time to develop a friendship strong enough to share Christ.

It's a proven fact that people don't want to open up their lives to strangers. Building friendships, however, allows us to bridge those barriers. With the investment in bridge-building friendships, the Holy Spirit can cross over to make the connection into a seeker's life. That's the power of relationally driven ministry.

It's also powerful in its potential for numbers. Even if Billy Graham reached a million people a year, it would take him over two centuries to reach the number of lost persons living right now in the United States. But if every believer reached just three people in a lifetime by effective witnessing, the lost in America would be reached within a generation.

CHAPTER 7

THE ISSUE GETS PERSONAL

Having left the corporate world and entered full-time ministry, I found that an important part of my new work was to search for allies. I continued to be involved with a wide range of church and ministry leaders across the United States. Throughout the next decade I worked closely with a number of parachurch ministries dedicated to evangelism, as well as with seminaries, Christian colleges, denominational offices, and other church agencies with a strong stake in training leaders to help churches reach the world for Jesus. From this perspective I gained a great deal of data about what was and was not happening in conversion evangelism.

What I learned was discouraging—in fact, downright depressing. The truth is there appeared to be little support and interest in reaching lost people for Jesus.

An example was a Christian conference center I worked with whose three major objectives were "to preach the Word of God, to nurture believers, and to reach lost people for Jesus." We brought in a teen ministry that did outreach to lost kids. On a typical weekend they brought in several hundred kids, of whom about 40 percent would make a first-time commitment of faith. But the conference center leaders raised strenuous objections when they found out some of these teens were actually smoking in the parking lots by the garbage Dumpsters. They were outraged that people with such "sinful" habits should be invited to the conference center. Over time, this objection to worldly or secular people, even in an honest attempt to introduce them to Jesus, caused the center's evangelism efforts to dry up.

I worked with Christian colleges and seminaries to try to introduce students to church-planting opportunities, but I was frustrated by the apparent fixation these institutions have on fund-raising. Equally eye-opening for me was my experience with evangelistic media ministries. These ministries raise millions of dollars to put the gospel message on the airwaves. Yet most of these programs, some of which are quite good, are carried on Christian radio stations. Why do these ministries spend millions of donor dollars to broadcast evangelism programs to an audience that's 96 percent Christian? The reason is quite simple: Doing so is critical for fund-raising from Christian audiences. The programs reach relatively few lost people, but both the radio stations and the evangelism ministries get a boost in donor income from Christian audiences who are grateful to see the gospel proclaimed.

Denominations I worked with also seemed to have little interest in pursuing efforts to jump-start evangelism and church growth. A key factor seemed to be a double standard that most of their churches seemed to follow, an observation pointed out to me by my friend Jeff Caliguire of Boston Sports Fellowship. The biblical mandate is to have low behavioral expectations for the unsaved while holding believers accountable to high standards. But most churches seem to have reversed this. Non-Christians aren't welcome until their lives are cleaned up and they conform to our church's cultural standards. In effect, they simply aren't welcome to join the family of God. But those already in the church can often exhibit the most sinful patterns of dysfunctional behavior with impunity.

ARRIVING NOWHERE

As the years went by after I'd left my marketing career, I had to evaluate my progress. After more than two decades of working with churches, denominations, and Christian agencies trying to stimulate more interest in going out into the woods to search for the spiritually lost (including my earlier side career as a church consultant before I moved to New England), where exactly had I arrived?

Nowhere. To be perfectly blunt and honest, I was at a dead end. I had to admit that I'd not found many people who were really interested in looking for the lost. Lots of people give the concept lip service, but very few actually do anything about it.

Over the years this reality increasingly dragged me down, eroded my faith, and left me with many questions about my experience of the

Christian life. It seemed so clear that Christ's Great Commission—to seek the lost and tell them the good news, to baptize new believers, make them into disciples, and teach them to disciple others—was a command for me. I'd wrestled for years to understand and obey this directive. But mostly I'd wrestled alone. I'd encountered others who saw the problem and understood some of its causes. No one I'd read about or heard of really had any solutions.

By the time I reached my early forties, I was discouraged, depressed, despairing. I could still clearly see the need for reaching the lost people in my life, in my community, and in my country. I'd tried everything I knew how to do, without a lot of success. I'd knocked on every door I could find in search of allies to help, without finding much interest.

The church reminded me of the spies sent to scout out the Promised Land in Numbers 13. Instead of believing God's promise of protection and empowerment to enable them to possess the Promised Land, they believed their own fears and weakness and spread a bad report among the people. The leaders of God's people simply didn't have the courage to follow, to trust, to obey. Their lack of faith led the whole people of God into sin. The result—God removed His blessing from His people, denied them the fulfillment of living in the Promised Land, and sentenced them to wandering in the desert until that whole generation died.

I really started to think that my life would end in despair. That's the fate I finally accepted. Like Moses, I had received the promise of a land of milk and honey, but I would never actually get to enter it myself. That privilege would fall to others after I was gone.

GOD AT WORK

And yet God wasn't finished with me. I continued to pray for the lost and to reach out to the few unsaved people I had a personal relationship with. The more I prayed, the more I began to hear one clear message from the Lord: *He cares about the lost.* It's true that our world has changed dramatically. It's true that strategies that once worked in reaching the lost no longer seem effective. It's true that few lost people are likely to come to church to find God, and that few believers from the church will go out into the world to look for them.

But as I prayed, God began to convince me that in spite of all these obstacles, He's still sovereign, and lost people really matter to Him. He began to convince me that He can deal with changing cultures and create new ways for His people to reach and enfold the lost.

To explain what God did next, I really need to say more about my friend and ministry partner, Dave Morgan.

Dave's a pastor. In fact, he's a third-generation pastor. His grandfather, Minot C. Morgan, was the senior pastor of the prestigious Fifth Avenue Presbyterian Church in New York City, one of the most famous pulpits of his day. Dave's father, Edward H. Morgan, graduated from Princeton University and Princeton Seminary, then became pastor of a large church in Philadelphia. After serving there for four years, he met the Lord Jesus Christ and committed his life to Him. His conversion had a profound impact on his life. For one thing, he was fired from his job at the church; the notion of his preaching the gospel was a little too radical for his congregation.

Edward Morgan then was called to be pastor of Westerly Road Church, a newly planted evangelical church in Princeton. He spent the remainder of his career serving this church, which became a beacon of light for the gospel amid the steady growth of liberalism at Princeton Seminary and in the churches in the Northeast.

I met Edward Morgan's son, David, at Gordon College. Dave went on to receive his master of divinity degree from Gordon-Conwell Theological Seminary, and later, as I've mentioned, he served as pastor of the church near Princeton that Martie and I helped plant. After leaving that church and moving to New Hampshire to work at The Leadership Center, he began to pastor a small, dying church of thirty-five people in his spare time. In less than ten years this church has grown to more than six hundred people.

Sounds like a classic success story, doesn't it? But Dave discovered that what looks like success ain't necessarily it.

Dave believes in the pastoral calling of the church. If I can paraphrase that philosophy, it would go something like this: *The goal of Christian ministry is to pastor and care for those who are willing to come to the church.* Given Dave's upbringing, experience, spiritual gifts, and experience of success, this is not an illogical philosophy for him to hold.

As long as we've known each other, Dave and I have ministered well together because we're opposites on many issues. My driving heart concern has always been for the outsider. My conviction is that the church's mission, and our individual mission as believers, is to go and share Jesus with others who don't yet know Him. My holding this philosophy of ministry is also not surprising, considering my own upbringing, experience, and spiritual gifts.

I was never able to sway Dave from his basic philosophy—until God made this whole issue very personal. Personal for my friend Dave, and, because of our deep friendship, very personal for me as well.

LEAVING HOME

Dave's oldest child, his only son, David B. Morgan Jr., delivered a wakeup call like no one else could have. Dave Jr. grew up in one of the best Christian homes in America. From childhood on, his parents have been models of sharing, teaching, and demonstrating Christ's love in their home. In addition, Dave Jr. had a lot of exposure to his grandparents, Ed and Betty Morgan, who are the most Christlike couple I've ever known. They lived nearby for most of Dave Jr.'s childhood and were a constant positive influence in his life. This boy also grew up in some of the best evangelical churches in America. Due to his father's gifts in leadership and teaching, young Dave was in nurturing, healthy churches during his childhood, youth, and teen years.

Then Dave Jr. reached eighteen and was graduating from high school. On the last day of Sunday school for the church year, typically in early June, our church has traditionally held a churchwide picnic after services to celebrate the end of the Sunday-school season and to encourage relationships in the family of God. During the church picnic on this particular year, Dave Jr. was chatting with his dad. He made an offhand comment that went something like this: "Well, thank God that's over! I've had enough Sunday-school classes to last me the rest of my life."

For my friend Dave, it was as if the world stood still. It was suddenly clear to him that his oldest child, his only son whom he loved dearly, was still at risk. He was not securely in the kingdom. He was graduating from high school and leaving home, and he wasn't fully committed to a relationship with Jesus as his Lord and Savior. If you've had children grow up under your influence and leadership and leave home (no matter what their condition on leaving), you can imagine and feel the terror that gripped my friend's heart.

For days, weeks, and months after this comment at a Sunday-school picnic, it was as if God was taking the scales off of Dave's eyes. He became aware of things he'd never seen before in his life. If the best of conventional Christian practices of our day hadn't worked for his son, were they even true? If the best that the traditional church had to offer wasn't effective at reaching his own son—who also came from a wonderful, warm, loving Christian home—how effective was it for all those young people who came from less-than-ideal home situations? How effective was it at reaching anyone at all?

The more Dave began to ask these painful questions, and to pray and to think, the more God opened him up to see new truths. Dave thought particularly about the people in his neighborhood. Yes, it was true that perhaps a half-dozen families from his street had come to church over the past decade and were now growing in relationships with Jesus. But there were at least two dozen more families that hadn't been touched by his church's ministry. They were open to the Morgans, open to relationships with Christians, and even interested in spiritual things. But they weren't the least interested in going to church.

Two neighbors in particular were increasingly in Dave's thoughts. Rick and Peter were about the same age, classic baby boomer families. Both men were still married to their first wives. Both couples were well educated, had good jobs, and several nice kids. They lived in nice homes, drove nice cars, and took care of their property—the ideal neighbors. Dave and his wife, Ruth, had good relationships with both families, and they enjoyed a good deal of openness in their friendships. Invite them to a picnic or cookout? Great! Invite them to church? Not a chance!

PROBING FOR ANSWERS

After that eye-opening experience in the summer of 1992, Dave and I began to spend a lot more time talking and praying about this problem. We read, we researched, we prayed, and we talked. We began to see the problem much more clearly but had no idea what the solution might be.

It was during this time that we read the book *Church Without Walls* by Jim Petersen. Petersen was a Navigator missionary who returned home from the mission field (in Brazil and elsewhere) and found the U.S. culture radically changed in relationship to the local church. He described how America has become a postmodern, post-Christian society. He concluded that much of our population is now a cross-cultural mission field—as much as those he experienced overseas—and unless the church takes major steps to reexamine its assumptions about lost people and how to win them, we won't reach the people of our generation. He identified major structural changes the church needs to make in its thinking and behavior to become an effective tool that God can use to reach lost people today.

Though Petersen's book seemed better at defining the problem than in proposing solutions, his probing, thoughtful critique played a major role in helping us discover the solutions to which God would lead us over the next few years.

CHAPTER 8

GOD'S SOLUTION

American Christianity's problem, as we've seen so far, can be stated quite simply:

- The majority of people in the United States are spiritually lost.
- Lost people are not going to come into our churches to find God.
- For the most part, traditional churches are not going to go out to search for them.

What is God's solution to this problem? Is His Word relevant to what we're dealing with today? In a drastically changing world, faced with ever-increasing numbers of people in our nation who appear to be drifting farther and farther from the ministry of the traditional local church, what can we do?

Not suprisingly, Scripture actually gives us excellent direction on how to cope with exactly the situation we face in America today.

GOD DOESN'T CHANGE, BUT HE CHANGES OUR PARADIGM

Yes, our world is changing. But change, of course, is no new phenome-non. If you look at the course of history—biblical and otherwise—you'll see that change is a constant. Attitudes, values, clothing, food, politics, economics, work, play—all are constantly changing.

What is God's response to all this change? God remains constant. He's constant in His love, constant in His grace, and constant in seeking to reconcile lost people to Himself. His principles for redemption and relationship are unchanging. But as people and cultures change, God alters not the principles of redemption but the *pattern* or *paradigm*—the forms, the structures, the cultural clothing. No matter what happens with lost people, God is ready with a new strategy to reach them.

God started human history with a personal, unhindered relation-ship with Adam and Eve. Their sin changed that relationship and brought about exile from the Garden of Eden. God responded with a new approach. In time He made a covenant with Noah and began building a new redemptive relationship with His people (Genesis 9).

Centuries later, following more changes in human culture, God called Abraham to Himself and initiated a covenant with him. Theolo-gians and historians note how God used the culturally relevant form of a binding legal agreement between kings—the suzerain treaty—as His model for this covenant. Unlike suzerain treaties, however, Abraham brought nothing to the covenant; he simply benefited from God's gra-cious offer and commitment to make from his descendants a tribe that would be God's special people (Genesis 15).

Later in Genesis we see God using Joseph to take the tribes of Israel to Egypt. There they multiplied and, through pain and hardship, were forged into a nation. Then we see God sending Moses to take them out and lead them to the Promised Land. There they became a settled, prosperous people with their own stable and unique social structure.

During this time God was also changing the pattern of worship for His people. While wandering in the desert of Sinai, they worshiped at the portable tabernacle, the "tent of meeting." When God's presence moved (as manifested in cloud and fire), the tabernacle and the people followed. In the Promised Land, as a settled people, they built a permanent temple in Jerusalem to serve as the "house of the Lord," all according to God's direction and design. People came from throughout Israel to worship Him at the temple.

More significant change came when God allowed His people to be conquered and sent into exile in Babylon. There the synagogue arose as a place for instruction in the Scriptures and for prayer. Even after the people were later restored to the land of Israel and the temple was rebuilt, the synagogues continued to function.

The most fundamental change came in the realization of the promised New Covenant, when the sacrificial form of worship at the temple was replaced with Jesus—the perfect, one-time sacrifice. Under this New Covenant, God now was living not in the temple but in the hearts of His people through the Holy Spirit—again, a major shift.

We see more big changes in Acts 10 and 15, as God moved quickly in supernatural ways (as well as through persecution) to push the first Jewish Christians out of their comfort zone. This was necessary to begin spreading the gospel to the Gentile world that surrounded these believers. Without this momentous shift, Christianity would still be a Jewish sect, and most of us would not be in the kingdom.

THE CHANGES CONTINUE

After the completion of the New Testament, church history continues to be replete with major changes ordained by God. One of the most revolutionary changes came to a head in the early sixteenth century after the "traditional model church" of that time—the Roman Catholic Church—had started running out of steam as an effective model. God raised up the Protestant Reformation, which became a major factor in spreading the gospel of Jesus Christ around the world just as new continents were opening to European exploration. The Reformation also, in time, provoked a renewal movement within the Catholic Church.

Later centuries saw the explosive rise of the modern missions movement worldwide as well as revivals and "awakenings" that led to waves of renewal, evangelism, and church growth. These significant paradigm shifts brought countless multitudes into the kingdom of God.

So throughout history, we see God respond to changing times and cultures to bring His unchanging redemption to people in fresh and relevant ways. God isn't frustrated by changing times and cultures, even if we are. He's steadfast in His desire to see men and women of every generation come into a saving relationship with Him through Jesus Christ. While the principles of redemption remain changeless, God keeps transforming the paradigm or patterns.

PROACTIVE INTERVENTION

Let's look back once more over history's big picture, and this time watch for the single theme of God's proactive intervention to rescue the lost. Whenever the people He created wandered deeper into the darkness of sin and disobedience, God didn't wait for them to come to their senses and return. He sent out a spokesman or a messenger to bring His children back.

We see this reflected in Abraham when he rescued his nephew Lot from Sodom and Gomorrah, and in Moses when he returned to Egypt to bring the people of Israel out from bondage. We see it in the book of Judges as God sent rescuers again and again to deliver His people from the consequences of their sin and disobedience. In King David, God sent a man after His own heart—only a lonely shepherd boy—to become a military and political leader to strengthen Israel's security in order that they might focus on worshiping the one true God. After the exile to Babylon, God continued to send such leaders and messengers as Daniel, Nehemiah, and Haggai to lead the people back to God.

Jesus is the ultimate illustration of God's principles of redemptive love in action. God sent His Son as a human being, knowing He would have to die, to reach out to the sin-darkened world. The sacrifice of His only Son was not too high a price to pay for bringing us home to the Father. And none of us had to first clean up our act and attain His righteous standards, which is what we often seem to expect the lost people of our era to do.

The parables Jesus told in Luke 15 reinforce this theme of active, redemptive love. The woman sweeping her whole house and searching everywhere until she finds her one lost coin represents God. So does the shepherd, willing to leave the warm, safe fold with the ninety-nine sheep in order to search the cold, dark, dangerous wilderness for his one lost lamb.

If we're to be God's incarnational feet and hands of love to our family, our friends, and our neighbors—to the lost people of our world—we need to be willing to sacrifice our comfort and go out. If we wait inside our comfort zone, inside the church (as many of us have done for years), hoping that the lost will simply come to us, we'll wait in vain. To be disciples of the One who came to call not the righteous but sinners, we must go out to the sick, lost, sin-damaged people of our day.

By his own example, Paul spells out the mission God gives us in 1 Corinthians 9:19-23:

> Though I am free and belong to no man, I make myself a
> slave to everyone, to win as many as possible. To the Jews I
> became like a Jew, to win the Jews. To those under the law I
> became like one under the law (though I myself am not
> under the law), so as to win those under the law. To those not
> having the law I became like one not having the law (though
> I am not free from God's law but am under Christ's law), so
> as to win those not having the law. To the weak I became
> weak, to win the weak. I have become all things to all men so
> that by all possible means I might save some. I do all of this
> for the sake of the gospel, that I may share in its blessings.

The modern missions movement has given us countless inspiring examples of believers who cared enough to leave their own comforts and their own world to risk everything to reach the lost. I think of Jim Elliot and his four friends who were murdered on the sands beside the Curaray River in Ecuador as they took the love of Jesus to the Auca Indians. Others followed in their courageous footsteps, and today thousands of the Aucas know Christ and follow Him.

Jim Rayburn's life is another powerful example. Jim was a youth pastor in a church in Dallas after World War II. No matter how hard he tried, he found that most kids in the local high school still would not come to church for his youth programs. In the spirit of the biblical shepherd seeking the lost sheep, Jim decided to take the gospel to those students—into the high school, onto the athletic fields, into their homes, wherever they hung out. That was the beginning of Young Life, a ministry to unchurched high-school kids that has reached millions of teens for Christ over the past fifty years.

Today, we too must be willing to leave behind our own culture and forms and comfort zones to go to the lost. Our goal is never to extract non-Christians out of their culture and pull them into ours, where they can be "Christians like us." Our goal is rather to plant an indigenous church—one that's culturally relevant—in that particular people group.

NEW-PARADIGM MINISTRIES

What is God's solution in today's America where the majority are spiritually lost, where they won't come to our churches to find Him, and where traditional churches for the most part are not going out to find them?

His solution is to raise up a new missionary force of people willing and able to go out to find lost people and be part of His eternal plan to rescue and redeem them into His family. *If people won't come to the church to find out about Jesus, then we are to take Jesus out of the church and go into the world of lost people.*

Today, God is at work all across America raising up a grass-roots movement of new-paradigm churches. They're springing up all over the landscape. One example is Pure Fun, which was started by a couple of young single Christians in Jonesboro, Arkansas, who were tired of spending Friday nights playing Nintendo and wanted a way to connect with other twenty-somethings. Now based in Mobile, Alabama, Pure Fun is led by Jason Wilke, who's at work jump-starting Pure Fun ministries all over the country.

Their approach is to start with a handful of Christians willing to organize fun, relational events twice a month and invite all their non-Christian friends. After six months of these events, they start an evangelistic Bible study with those who are interested. New converts and committed Christians are then invited to a discipleship Bible study.

Another example is Boston Sports Fellowship. It was founded by Jeff and Mindy Caliguire, a young couple who came to Boston in the early 1990s to plant a Willow Creek–style church—a seeker-sensitive, traditional church model. But this model didn't work well in Boston. God led the Caliguires instead to reach out and build relationships with people who have a love for sports and adventure. Boston Sports Fellowship now reaches young professionals, some single, some married, some with kids, and some without. They form friendships in the context of their sports adventures, and the friendships lead to commitments to Christ. New believers are enfolded into small groups where they discover Christian community. As they mature, they go on to become a full part of the church and the ministry team.

Ministries like these are effectively reaching out to people who aren't being reached by more traditional methods. I'm certainly not aware of all of them or even most of them, but I've seen or heard of quite a few over the past decade. They take on a number of forms and have a variety of approaches in ministry. But they do have some important characteristics in common.

1. New-paradigm churches tend to be focused on a group of unreached people rather than on a geographic location. Rather than sending a person or a team to plant a church in East Overshoe, Ohio, the new-paradigm churches focus on a group of people of a certain age, or in a certain stage in life, or with some other common attributes or needs that make them distinct as a group.

2. New-paradigm churches are driven by relational networks rather than by buildings or programs. They work through people's natural connections to other people rather than asking everyone to come to a central location for a programmed event.

3. New-paradigm churches are most often lay-driven and lay-led. For decades the evangelical church has struggled, without

much success, with the issue of how to activate the laity and mobilize them into the ministry of the local church. Now the new-paradigm churches are doing it. They have a biblical view grounded in the doctrines of spiritual gifts, universal servant-hood, and the priesthood of all believers that frees all of the body of Christ for service and ministry.

CHAPTER 9

TURNING POINT

At one point during the years Dave and I were earnestly praying and searching, the church we were part of had a strategic planning retreat for its leaders. Among others, that included Dave and me—Dave was serving as senior pastor, and I was the head of our church council (equivalent to a team of elders or a board of overseers).

In analyzing the church's ministry opportunities in the surrounding communities, the conclusion we as a group arrived at was that our church was reaching only about 20 percent of the people who lived in these areas. That's how many people were realistically open to the church and willing to attend. Eighty percent of the population in our area of ministry seemed to be quite closed to the church and unwilling to come there to hear about God or for any other reason. They were culturally resistant to the church. That 80-to-20 ratio closely matched Dave's analysis of the openness toward his church among people in the neighborhood where he lived.

So what were we to do with that finding?

Much to my surprise, the conclusion the church council reached was that we ought to forget the 80 percent and focus on the 20 percent. Yes, we knew about God's heart for the lost—all of them matter deeply to God, and He wants to bring them into relationship with Him. But we simply didn't know how to reach that 80 percent. Dave and I were both very well read on evangelism and church growth, and we didn't know. Many others had identified similar problems elsewhere and could only describe why the old proven methods no longer worked.

Besides, even reaching the 20 percent gave us lots of growth problems. We needed more space, more rooms, more parking, and more staff to try to service all the people who were already coming into the church.

So as a council we decided to forget the 80 percent. We didn't know what to do to reach them, so God would have to take care of them. Several members of the council objected to this callous disregard for the great majority of the people in our communities, but we simply didn't know how to reach out to them.

For the next two or three years, we moved forward with the church's agenda while Dave and I continued to talk, read, and pray together. We searched the bookshelves of Christian bookstores hoping to find the answer. We talked to church leaders all over the country and attended conferences and seminars looking for the answers…without success.

In the winter of 1994–95, our church had grown to the point that a new building was absolutely vital for the ministry to grow. This need triggered a violent "pioneer-homesteader" conflict (as church building proposals so often do). While the great majority of the church favored moving forward and building new facilities, a small handful of old-timers refused to budge. They didn't want the church to be a regional church (though at the time it served people from twenty-eight different towns). They felt it wouldn't be so bad to get rid of all the new "outsiders" while we were at it. Congregational votes on the new building came in at one hundred in favor and six opposed, yet still we couldn't move forward. The conflict was so great, it appeared the church would split.

In January of 1995, a group of people began to meet weekly to pray for the situation in the church, which had grown quite serious. While some were in favor of healing the division in the church, others were praying that God would release us to go off and plant a new regional church. As we prayed, it became clear that God was saying, "Don't plant a new regional church to reach the people that are already being reached. Go start something new to reach the 80 percent the church isn't reaching."

OUR RESPONSIBILITY

The more we began to look at our world from God's perspective, the more we began to see our situation in a new light. The more we thought and prayed about the problem we'd identified, the more personal the issue became.

It wasn't just that there are as many as two hundred million spiritually lost people in America and the church doesn't know how to reach them. It wasn't just that 80 percent of the people in the different towns our church served were beyond the reach of the ministries of our congregation. It wasn't just that seven out of ten people we know at work and in our neighborhood stand a pretty high chance of spending eternity shut out of the presence of their loving heavenly Father. All of these issues were important to consider, but they weren't the most important.

What really began to motivate us was the thought that some of these people who could be lost for eternity were living in our own homes or were members of our extended families. They were some of our best friends, some of our favorite people from our workplace. They were the neighbors who looked after our kids for years and fed our pets when we were on vacation.

We were thinking about people we'd known for years. People we loved and cared about. People we hadn't really shared our faith with in a very effective manner. Oh, sure, we had prayed that they would come to know Jesus. When we could, we invited them to go to church with us, if we weren't embarrassed that it might turn them off to God. But most of them simply had no interest in going to church—good, bad, or indifferent.

Frankly, there's nothing on earth I care about more than being together with my wife and kids at God's party in eternity. There's nothing I wouldn't pay or sacrifice to ensure that we're all together with God for all time. I feel the same concern for my friends and other people I care about. I want to be friends with them for eternity, not just for this year or this life. I want them to discover God's best for now and for eternity. And I don't want to face them at the beginning of eternity and have to say, "I never told you about Jesus because I really didn't care enough about you, and I was too absorbed in my own pursuits."

The more we prayed and thought about this issue from this personal perspective, the harder it became to simply put it down and walk away. It became clear that these lost people whom God kept bringing to mind might somehow be our personal responsibility. If *I* wasn't the person God would use to bring my kids to faith, who did I think was going to do the job?

When I thought through the list of non-Christian people God had already put in my life, I realized that for most of them I was the closest person to them who knew Jesus. For some I was the *only* person they knew who was in touch with Jesus. If I was unwilling to tell them about Jesus and how to find eternal life through Him, who was going to tell them? When we arrive in eternity and God is sorting out the people to go to heaven and hell, and I see these friends getting ready to go to an eternity without God, what will I say? When they look me in the eye and say, "Why didn't you ever tell me about Jesus?" how will I answer? How will I feel? I might have been the one and only means God gave them to join His family, yet I never did anything about it.

It simply wouldn't cut it to say, "Well, I wanted to help them, but I could never get them to go to church with me." Or "I wanted to help, but our church council voted to go a different direction." Or "I wanted to help, but I didn't know what to do or how to do it. So I did absolutely nothing."

MORE THAN WILLING

As we asked God to show us what He wanted us to do, He began to convince us that He could teach us how to work with Him to reach out to these friends with Jesus' love. We didn't have to wait for the church to develop an effective new ministry. We didn't have to wait for a parachurch ministry to send a staff worker to reach these people. We didn't even have to try to convince our friend to come to church with us. The church wasn't even a relevant issue to the problem.

As God continued to give us new light, it became clear that the issue was not how to connect a person to the church. The issue was *how can I connect my friend to Jesus?* Only by establishing a personal relationship with Jesus will our friends ever begin to discover new life in Christ. The journey of faith begins only with a personal introduction to Jesus. Sometimes the church helps in that; sometimes it doesn't. The church really makes a difference in eternity only when it connects people to Jesus and encourages people to trust Him and walk with Him each day.

So we started with a clean sheet of paper. Dave and I were meeting at least once a week for a couple hours to pray and brainstorm. We literally took blank pads of paper and prayed, "Lord, show us what you would have us do about the lost people you've put in our lives." As God spoke, we would talk, share, put ideas on paper, then pray some more.

God convinced us that He could provide everything we needed to share our faith effectively with our kids, our family members, our friends, and our neighbors. Week after week, He gave us clear and simple insights from His Word and from our own experiences in ministry about how we could build relationships and share Jesus with those who were outside the reach of our church or other ministries.

As Dave and I began to share this new light with other believers, the response was remarkable! We found that people were more than willing to take responsibility for individuals God had placed in their lives, if only someone would teach them what to do.

So it was that the ministry we call New Life came into being—not through some brilliant strategy we came up with and implemented with remarkable human genius, but out of the ferment and anguish in our church situation, and with a lot of prayer, brainstorming, and developmental thinking, all guided by the direction we sensed from the Lord.

GETTING STARTED

We began the ministry in June of 1995 with about thirty people who were interested in responding to the call to "do something new" to reach the lost people in their lives that the church couldn't reach. Our goal was to figure out how to get from where we were as believers to where we needed to be to reach the spiritually lost. How could we take Christians from traditional model churches and turn them into cross-cultural missionaries with the ability to reach and disciple "culturally unchurched" secular people in the world they live in?

Dave and I continued to meet and pray and talk. We prayed, "What should we do first, Lord?"

That summer we ran a seven-week training course for this first group of interested "New Lifers." During the course, we went back to the basics—like new coach Vince Lombardi in his first practice session with the Green Bay Packers, when he held the ball up and said, "This is a football!" That was our approach as well.

It was amazing how little this group of committed, motivated, and longtime Christians knew of the basics of the Christian life. These folks had been in the church for years. Many were leaders—pillars of the church. It became clear as we worked through those first sessions that there was a fundamental flaw in the church's thinking. Here we'd been giving some of the best preaching and teaching from the pulpit week after week, year after year, under the assumption that people were catching on and applying these eternal truths to their lives. It just wasn't true. They hadn't looked as though they were asleep, but their ability to understand, apply, and implement these teachings in their lives was much lower than we thought.

As we continued teaching through that summer of 1995, we kept asking the question, "What basic skills do believers have to know to be effective missionaries to their friends?" This question was examined from a lot of different perspectives. One Sunday in a discussion in the car with my teenage daughters, they put the issue this way: "If the government closed down all the churches in America, what would a Christian have to do to maintain and spread his faith in Jesus?"

Our discussions kept coming back to five basic skills we felt would be needed to make someone a good cross-cultural missionary.

The first skill was *nurturing and developing your own relationship with God.* If you aren't growing spiritually yourself, you probably don't have anything worth sharing with your non-Christian friends. If you aren't spiritually healthy yourself, you probably won't share, because you're embarrassed at how little positive influence Jesus is having in your own life.

The second skill was *dealing with issues of culture.* Communicating and living in a highly secular culture raises all kinds of boundaries between Christians and non-Christians. If we were sending you overseas to another culture as a missionary, you might get two years of language and culture training before you began ministry. Our situation here is no different. Most believers need considerable training in dealing with cultural issues before they can effectively communicate with non-Christians.

Building effective relationships was the third skill we began to focus on. We were amazed at how little most Christians know about how to build an effective friendship, and we were surprised that some of these people still had intact marriages. So we focused on building strong, positive relationships, on learning how to communicate effectively, and on developing relationships with the potential for spiritual growth.

The fourth skill was *sharing your faith with someone else.* This included teaching believers to share their story and the gospel and to know how to help a person negotiate the transaction as the Holy Spirit leads them to faith.

Teaching evangelism yielded some especially interesting results. For years I'd taught and spoken on the topic of evangelism and developed a reputation of having some expertise in this area. But trying to practically teach these New Lifers about evangelism opened up insights and understanding for me that twenty-five years of experience never had.

We realized clearly that so much of what has gone wrong with evangelism in the American church is because of the wrong methods we've used. So in New Life we emphasized that you don't have to have the spiritual gift of evangelism to be effective at sharing your faith. (The Bible teaches the same thing.) We taught them how to understand and negotiate the cultural differences of a secular person. We taught them how to build an effective relationship and over time to move it into spiritual conversations, and then to be ready to share their own story and the essentials of the gospel, in five minutes or less.

We urged them to practice. We taught them that their story and the gospel were like their six-shooters in the Wild West. You had to practice enough so you could get them out of the holsters when you needed them! It is this preparation and practice that the Holy Spirit uses to help people come to faith in Jesus.

The final skill we taught was *nurturing a new believer.* Just as a new parent has to learn how to care for and nurture their own child, believers need to learn how to nurture the spiritual growth and development of new followers of Jesus.

These were the topics we taught our people about life with God and Jesus and the Holy Spirit. None of it was really new. It was just the basics—basics that we'd always assumed Christians had and were using in their Christian lives, but basics that most believers today simply don't have.

CHAPTER 10

PRIORITIES
DO MATTER

In themselves, those five skills that we were teaching our people were not the most important discovery God led us to that first summer in 1995. In fact, we really didn't boil down the list of five skills into its final form until we'd been teaching for eighteen months.

The more important issue God led us to during that summer was that of priorities. It would be easy to look at those five skills and say, "Most Christians know something about these skills and have for years. How will focusing on them make a dramatic difference in anyone's life?" The truth is, skills alone won't make a dramatic difference in people's lives, let alone their ability to share their faith. But a change in *priorities* makes a profound and dramatic difference in shaping lives.

The power of priorities is probably the most important lesson God has taught us through the New Life process. When we explain the New Life ministry to others, we like to focus on three aspects—the ministry's *priorities,* its *principles,* and its *practices.* Each is important, but the most important is the priorities, followed by principles, and only then by practices.

In our ministry's first year, we saw a 30 percent growth in numbers through conversion evangelism—sixteen new converts reached by our group of fifty believers. I'm convinced that the reason for this high rate of fruitfulness flows from the *priorities* of our model. New Life is built with garden-variety Christians, a range of people pretty typical of those you would find in any church—a few are mature believers; many are not. Most don't have the spiritual gift of evangelism. In fact, very few do. And yet our ministry model has proven to be incredibly fruitful because these people have made sharing their faith a priority.

These are people who truly believe that lost people matter to God and that He can use them and their friendships to win people to Jesus. They pray, "Lord, whom should I reach out to and befriend? Whom should I pray for?" They listen to God, then pray and act in specific relationships with specific people.

They're people who are equipped to build effective relationships—relationships that lead to trust, communication, and spiritual exploration.

They're people who know how to share, simply and effectively, the gospel and their own story of faith.

They're people who know how to nurture and disciple new believers.

They're people in committed community with other like-minded believers, being supported and held accountable in their walk with Jesus and in their relationships with others.

And they're people who regularly see God act. When we come together each month for a time of celebration and hear how God has miraculously brought another person into the family or miraculously changed a person's life, we're not only encouraged, but we also believe that God can reach *our* friends too.

Priorities do matter! They make all the difference in the outcomes produced by different church models.

WHAT GETS DONE FIRST?

That word *priorities* is just another way of saying, "What gets done first?" When a church sets priorities, it answers questions like these:

- What's really essential to our faith?
- What should we do first?
- What should we do best?
- Whom are we trying to impress?
- Whom are we trying to make comfortable?

Priorities are critical because they shape the outcome of different church models. Though rarely mentioned and too seldom debated in the church, priorities make all the difference in the world. Priorities determine what will actually *result* from a ministry's efforts. They determine what actually gets taken care of in a world with too many needs and demands and not enough time and resources.

If I pay my tithe to the Lord out of the money I have left over at the end of the month, the Lord isn't going to get very much (let alone 10 percent). But if I make the Lord my first priority in my finances (the biblical concept of firstfruits) and pay my tithe first, before I pay any other bills, the Lord will stand a lot better chance of actually getting what I want to give Him.

TWO DIFFERENT MODELS

Let me illustrate how priorities shape the outcome of church models by showing you two different church models, both of which are biblical. As we discussed earlier, the New Testament illustrates a wide variety of church structure and form. Each model simply illustrates a different set of ways to go about trying to accomplish what God intends the church to accomplish.

The first diagram is the traditional church model, the model most of us are familiar with:

THE TRADITIONAL MODEL

Acts 2:24

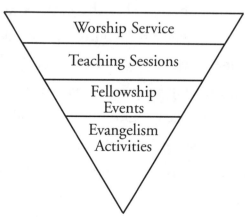

102

We find support for this traditional model in the example of the early church in Acts 2:42: "They devoted themselves to the apostles' teaching and to the fellowship, to the breaking of bread and to prayer." The first (most important) priority is the Sunday morning worship service. In most churches, this function takes up the major share of people, resources, and time. According to this model, the less important functions—teaching, fellowship, and evangelism—are approached in such a way that they don't conflict or interfere with the worship service.

Under this traditional model, most of a believer's active involvement in the Christian life is taken up by attending meetings or events in the company of other Christians.

Dr. Donald McGavran and Dr. Peter Wagner, after years of research on churches in America, arrived at the conclusion that most local churches have used up between 90 and 95 percent of their talent, time, and money before they get to the last priority—evangelism.

This is a model suited especially for a society with mostly Christian values and a basic understanding of Christianity—in particular, the kind of rural parish culture that was dominant in America and Europe many long decades ago. After all, why spend a large share of your resources on evangelism in a society where almost everyone is already a Christian, or at least knows the gospel?

New Life is based on another model that finds support in the Great Commission Jesus gave His disciples: "Therefore go and make disciples of all nations, baptizing them in the name of the Father and of the Son and of the Holy Spirit, and teaching them to obey everything I have commanded you" (Matthew 28:19-20). The following diagram illustrates this model's priorities.

NEW LIFE MODEL

Matthew 28:18-20

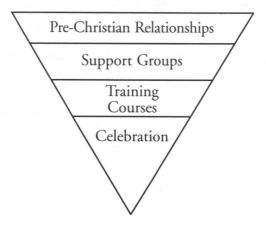

The number one priority of believers in the New Life model is to start bridge-building relationships with "pre-Christians" (nonbelievers) that can lead to spiritual growth. We encourage our people to think of the total time they have available for spiritual and ministry activities and then to spend at least half of it building the kind of relationships with pre-Christians that can have spiritual potential. All other "church" functions are designed to follow and support this top priority.

Clearly, it's easier for God to use us to reach nonbelievers if we're spending plenty of time with them. To commit that time to them usually means dropping out of many fellowship opportunities and other responsibilities in our local church.

It only makes sense to place a high priority on evangelism when you're a small minority in a thoroughly secular and even hostile culture. This is a church model designed for times like—well, like the twenty-first century here in America.

Both the traditional church model and our New Life model share many elements. The traditional worship service corresponds at least loosely to our New Life "celebrations." The same broad connection exists between traditional teaching sessions and our training courses, traditional fellowship events and our support groups, and traditional evangelism and our "pre-Christian relationships." But these elements are prioritized quite differently in each model, and that difference radically impacts their outcome.

Let me ask you two questions.

1. *If your sanctuary burned down, how long would it take your church to find an alternate place to hold Sunday worship services?* If yours is like most churches, it would take about one week. And in only twelve to eighteen months (that's the national average), your sanctuary would be rebuilt so you could again hold worship services in your own building. Why? Because Sunday worship is the most important thing we do! Nothing else comes close. No matter what it costs or what it takes, we want to be back at worship as soon as possible.

2. *If evangelism didn't happen in your church, how long would it take for people to get upset and finally do something about it?* Let's be honest. Evangelism isn't happening to any great degree in most

of our churches, and it hasn't been for a long time. Few people have gotten upset over this, and even fewer have done anything about it. Why? Evangelism is not really a top priority. We might say it is, but in fact, it isn't.

And that's why there's been no appreciable increase in the number of born-again Christians in America within living memory. That's why 80 percent of our churches are stagnant or declining. Evangelism is simply not a priority for our churches—and *priorities do matter!*

BREAKING THROUGH THE WALL

Most traditional churches exist behind a boundary or wall that clearly delineates who's "in" and who's "out" of the church. It's the fortress mentality. Most of the people inside the church are facing inward. They have an inward agenda and aren't inclined to hang out or build friend-

NONGROWING CHURCH

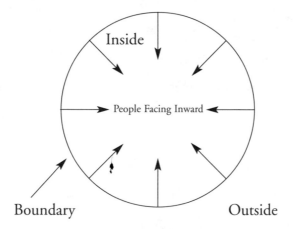

ships with non-Christians. Few are deliberately seeking to build bridges to the lost, and other than the pastor, few are equipped to share Christ. But the pastor is usually fully occupied with his work in the church and with the congregation, and he has limited opportunities to build relationships with non-Christians. The result is usually a church that is growing slowly or not at all.

Other churches have more permeable boundaries to various degrees, with greater numbers of people who exhibit a relational evangelism lifestyle. Some churches develop small-group ministries, counseling or healing ministries, or other types of outwardly focused programs that create more opportunities for developing relationships with non-Christians, and these eventually lead to conversion evangelism. Others create "fishing" events—programs run in the environment of the non-Christian in order to stimulate relational development between believers and others.

PERMEABLE BOUNDARIES

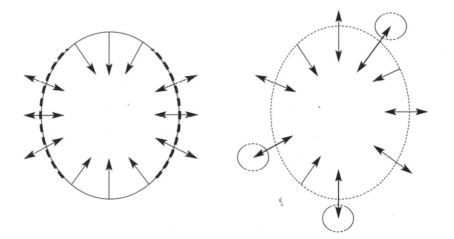

The New Life approach pushes this boundary-breaking to the extreme. It eliminates—or blurs—the boundary that defines who's in the church and who's outside so that you have to connect to a person and learn about his or her relational network (through support teams and celebration groups) to determine where the "church" is.

This model creates tremendous opportunities for relationships with pre-Christians. The high degree of relational exposure and the lower level of boundaries contribute to more effectiveness in evangelism.

Perhaps the best way to picture this model is as an organic compound. Each believer is represented by a dot and each pre-Christian friend is represented by an X. Structurally, it might look something like this:

NEW LIFE MODEL OF RELATIONAL NETWORKS

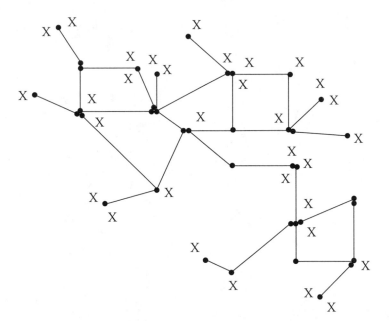

The key to successful evangelism and discipleship in any church model today is effective relationships. Younger generations are disconnected, fragmented, isolated, lonely. Many find their only friends on television programs or on the Internet. They're not only spiritually hungry and open, they're relationally hungry. One of their most noted traits is their innate distrust of institutions and of cognitive lectures on "what is truth." They're much more open to hearing truth through relationships with others.

CHAPTER 11

PROVEN IMPACT

———————

My wife, Martie, works in a public elementary school as an instructional specialist teaching children with learning problems how to read. God has given her a tremendous heart of compassion for the kids she works with, many of whom are very needy and come from the difficult circumstances often found amid rural poverty. The staff at this school are highly skilled and caring professionals who are truly motivated by the opportunity to make a difference in children's lives.

Because it's a public school, talking about God with the children isn't allowed, as is consistent with the politically correct environment of public education today. Even if a child is open and interested in learning more about Jesus, it simply can't be done in the school setting. School administrators are terrified about lawsuits and the liability that might arise should anyone complain about religious faith being promoted in a public school setting.

Our first group of New Life trainees included two other teachers who worked at Martie's school. Throughout the training they talked about how God might be able to use them and their newfound skills to minister at the school.

FRUITFUL FRIENDSHIPS

Susan, one of the teachers, began to build a friendship with Liza, another teacher at the school. In the process of building a trust relationship, Susan asked Liza if she would consider taking a trip with her to Ireland during summer vacation. Liza was thrilled. Her husband was a steady but quiet guy who had little interest in traveling. Liza, like Susan, wanted to travel but wasn't willing to go alone. After planning their trip throughout the winter and spring, they spent three weeks in the summer exploring the Emerald Isle. Their time together on the trip enabled them to build a firm foundation of friendship and trust. After returning, Susan continued to build the relationship as Liza became more open to discussing spiritual issues.

Nine months later, Liza's relationship with Jesus became real in a new way. Another nine months after that, her husband, Mack, also began to walk with Jesus. Both Liza and Mack are now blossoming and growing in their Christian life.

Other opportunities for ministry at the school arose after a first-grade boy was struck and killed by a car while one of his playmates stood by in horror and watched it happen. The school authorities went through the usual drill for dealing with this type of situation, but the New Life women got together before school to pray for the kids and their families and all those coping with this tragedy. Several women who weren't believers asked if they could come and participate. Later they asked Martie and her friends to start a regular group after school where they could learn more about the Bible and have the chance to pray about issues that came up in their lives. Eventually a regular support group began. Each of the New Lifers invited staff members they had friendships with, those they sensed might be open to God. Others simply heard about it through the grapevine and asked if they could come. This gathering was the beginning of a New Life "cell," where seekers feel comfortable enough to explore a relationship with God.

Paula is a reading teacher who got involved with this support group and soon made a personal commitment to Jesus. She has continued to grow in her faith through this group and, with her two school-age kids, is now actively growing through the ministry of a local church.

Sharon was a new teacher in her early twenties. Full of life and enthusiasm, she was fun to be with and a great teacher for young children. After participating in the support group for a number of months she commented,

> I have gone to church all my life. I attended as a child, then
> I taught Sunday school. I was married in the church, and
> my husband and I still go to church with my parents. How
> is it I have never heard any of this stuff about Jesus? I feel
> like I got ripped off!

Sharon eventually made a commitment to Jesus and started to grow in faith. She invited her mother and her aunt to various activities the support group sponsored. First her aunt and then her mother made faith commitments. They joined the group and are continuing to grow.

A different kind of ministry opportunity opened up with June, a third-grade teacher who had married late and had a child, and who struggled with control and fear issues in her life. Martie and two of her friends had a good relationship with June, and they invited her to join them for a four-day trip to New York City after school was out. They explored museums, went to Broadway shows, and enjoyed some shopping. In the process a number of spiritual conversations took place, but June didn't make a commitment to Jesus on that trip.

Two years later, after moving with her family to Texas, June wrote to her friends. She described the rest of the process God had led her through until she reached the point of trusting in Jesus. The turning point in her journey to faith, she said, had been that four-day trip with her friends to New York.

SOMETIMES MORE SLOWLY

Over the past few years at this school, God has used Martie and her two New Life friends to help eight to ten people come to Christ—all in this one workplace situation. Some have come to faith quickly, after demonstrating obvious spiritual hunger and specific questions about God. Others have come to faith slowly and gradually in a process of tiny, incremental changes over the years.

Emily had been a teacher at the school for more than twenty-five years and had become an influential leader in the school and in her community. She began attending the support group regularly, but for two years she never said a thing while she was there.

Finally, at one of the group's last meetings before summer vacation, she spoke up:

> I was raised Catholic. Faith was simply not something you
> shared about with other people. Kevin and I have been
> married for over twenty-five years and have shared every-
> thing, and yet I have never talked with him about faith.
> Even though I never say anything in these meetings, I want
> you to know that God has been working in my life, and my
> trust in Him is growing.

Several weeks later, during a summer afternoon thunderstorm, lightning struck Emily's home—an antique colonial house that she and Kevin had spent twenty-five years restoring. They were away on vacation with their children when they got the news. She arrived back in time to watch the firemen put out the last smoldering embers of what had been her home, now burned to the ground.

We were terrified about how this tragedy might have a negative impact on Emily's faith. But her first reaction was an outpouring of heartfelt thanks to the local firemen, many of whom had been her students in elementary school. She walked around to personally thank each one for coming to her family's aid.

As she and Kevin surveyed the charred ruins, she thanked God that they'd been gone when the lightning hit. The bolt hit the room where one of her sons did his summer reading each afternoon. Had they been home when the lightning struck, her son's life might have been taken. She was grateful to God they had lost only a house.

In short, this tragedy became an opportunity for Emily's young faith to grow and mature. Her friends from the support group rallied around and helped her through the long process of rebuilding. They delivered God's message of love, caring, and hope in real and tangible ways.

HELPING YOU REACH YOUR FRIENDS

These are just a few stories from one small group in one New Life ministry. There are many other exciting stories of how God is able to use the New Life process to help ordinary people begin to share in the extraordinary things He wants to do through our lives to reach lost people for Jesus.

When Christians ask me, "What is New Life?" I don't tell them, "It's a new-paradigm church designed to reach those beyond the reach of the traditional church"—even though that's true. I tell them that it's a missionary strategy to help believers reach their friends who won't go to church.

When they ask me to tell them more, I describe the three major benefits Christians receive from being a part of New Life:

1. New Life offers an innovative way to experience the abundant life that Jesus promises all believers.

2. New Life provides simple but very effective ways to share the good news of Jesus Christ with family, friends, and neighbors.

3. New Life allows our friends who become Christians to grow into true maturity in Christ. Our goal in New Life goes beyond evangelism. That's just one point in a process that God has planned for each person. Our goal is to "present every [person] mature in Christ" (Colossians 1:28, RSV) so that we will grow up into the mature, reproducing believers God intended us to be all along (Matthew 28:18-20). We become fully authentic Christians in the real world of our everyday life—not just on Sunday at church. We take hold of the right priorities that enable us to simplify our lifestyle and schedule, bringing sanity to the too-busy world most of us live in and enabling us to maximize the impact of Christ in our home, in our extended family, in our neighborhood, and at work.

COMMITMENT TO COMMUNITY

As we taught our first group of New Lifers during that summer of 1995, another critical lesson we learned had to do with *how* we teach. We discovered that teaching people new skills in a cognitive sense wasn't going to change anyone's life.

This discovery contradicted our deeply held assumption that the key to change is to absorb new information. Our educational system is based on that notion—the more "learning" you've been exposed to, the more competent you're supposed to be. The higher the volume of "learning," the higher the degree. It's the system our seminaries use: Expose a person to a large enough body of theological and ministry information, and you make him qualified to lead a congregation. It's the system our churches are based on: Expose people to enough biblical information through sermons or Christian education, and you make them mature, reproducing followers of Christ.

Even our society recognizes the fallacy in this view. For positions that *really matter,* society won't accept exposure to cognitive information alone as the basis for competency. To be licensed as a doctor or an airplane pilot you must also complete a rigorous process of mentoring and hands-on learning under a skilled practitioner. In fact, the mentoring usually takes far more time and effort than does the book learning.

Even ordinary people who simply want to drive a car have to do more than pass a test on cognitive knowledge. They usually go through a mentoring stage as a student driver with a learner's permit under the oversight of a more experienced driver, and they must pass a test to demonstrate actual competence behind the wheel before they're licensed to drive on their own.

In skills that really matter, society insists on much more than cognitive learning as a basis for expertise. In areas that we've decided don't really matter—such as being a professor of sociology or a pastor of a church—well, then, practical experience and mentoring and real world competence don't have to be part of the equation.

As we taught the basic New Life skills, we realized we were taking people who had never been disciples and were trying to teach them how to become disciplers so they could lead others into a mature relationship with Jesus. How do you teach someone to be a discipler who has never been discipled? It was a tough question, and we knew the answer was *not* to teach them a body of cognitive knowledge.

We went back to God in prayer. The answer God gave us was to put people into small groups and let the *group* itself disciple each of the individuals in it. By combining the strengths and gifts and experiences of each person, we found that the small group could function almost like a mature Christian in a discipleship role with each person. As people grew in this way, they would be able to disciple others.

THE POWER OF SMALL GROUPS

Gary Smalley is one of many Christian leaders who says small groups are the most effective way to help people change. "I've tried and seen others try lots of ways to try to help adults change," Smalley writes, "but small groups are still the most powerful tool."

A healthy small group can actually re-parent us. It's a safe place where people don't induce blame or shame. There's the freedom to talk, to think, to feel, to get connected to others so we can know that we're loved. Such a group, Smalley says, "if it is purpose-driven, gives us the energy to stay committed to our purposes. It gives us the hope and encouragement we need to go on."[7]

That's exactly what we've found with the support teams in New Life. Besides the family-like love and security it offers, and the positive role models from other believers who are caring for lost friends, it provides a source of energy and hope and encouragement as we pursue God's work of evangelism and discipleship among secular people in America today.

This experience led us into more discoveries on the whole concept of community, one of the most important elements that we've discovered in New Life. Character, we've learned, can only be shaped in community. We've found that you really need to be involved in community to become a doer of God's Word and not just a hearer. Many Christian leaders have tried to teach people evangelism and discipleship skills, only to see the whole thing die down after the training was over and people were out on their own where other issues in life distracted them. Community is so often the missing critical factor. Nothing else can do as much to help people claim God's truth and make it their own.

When we first considered starting small groups with the people from that first summer's training course, we found that most of the participants had little natural affinity for one another. They were all interested in the training and the cause, but not in the personalities sitting around them.

To solve this, we told them to go out and recruit other people to start a small group with. If you were a couple, you needed to find at least one other couple to commit to your group. If you were a single, you had to find at least two other singles to join you.

Since then, the New Life teams that have developed are specialized small groups with a purpose. They usually range from five to twelve people, while the average is probably six or eight. These small teams provide their members with personal support, nurture, and heart-to-heart friendships. In the context of these small groups is where pastoral care in the New Life model takes place. It's also where we find practical support and accountability as we try to reach out in love to befriend pre-Christian people. The teams also provide prayer cover—prayer for us as individuals, prayer for the specific people we're caring for, and prayer for the whole New Life ministry.

These teams are *not* Bible study groups, or teaching times, or cell churches, or an evangelistic outreach, or support groups focused on working through personal problems. Instead, their purpose is to nurture supportive relationships for individuals who want to pray for and reach out to lost people.

These groups are the primary place where such believers can be plugged in relationally to a greater fellowship. This is where they can be known, share intimately, and receive support in times of suffering and hardship. It's also the primary place for accountability and support in our individual efforts to build friendships, share the gospel, and disciple new believers. The groups provide ongoing training and Bible study with a focus on the five fundamental skills taught in our basic training course, which all New Lifers are required to go through.

In short, these teams provide the context of community that every Christian needs to live and minister effectively.

BARBARA'S STORY

Barbara's story demonstrates the power of community. Barbara was in her early eighties when she decided to take the New Life training. (Don't ask me why; it sure wasn't designed for people in that age group.) A godly woman, she'd been raised in a Christian home, had made an early commitment to Christ, and had married a man who became a pastor. She and her husband put Christ's love into action and had a long and fruitful ministry in the local church before her husband died.

We told Barbara that our New Life approach might not be an appropriate strategy for her, and that most of her friends would probably be more receptive to the ministry of our local church. She came to our training anyway. She recruited a group of contemporaries—about ten people between the ages of fifty-five and seventy-five—and started her own team. This group consistently attended any training we offered and continued meeting faithfully as a small group.

I asked Barbara what she was getting out of New Life that she hadn't already experienced from her seventy years as a believer. She told me that in the environment of their small group,

> Learning about the needs of the lost and praying for specific
> people is really changing my perspective on lost people. I
> see them much more clearly than I ever did before. I under-
> stand their situation and feel I have a much better sense of
> what part I play in God's desire to help them.

Barbara volunteered in the elder care program of a local hospital. Several days a week she spent a few hours helping needy seniors who attended the program on a walk-in, day-care basis. Cindy, the professional staff person running the program, seemed open to a close relationship with Barbara, so Barbara prayed and made an effort to befriend her. Cindy began to open up and share. She was in her midthirties when her marriage had fallen apart, and she'd walked out of the relationship and gotten involved in a lesbian relationship. She was now living with her lesbian partner.

Barbara was shocked by these revelations, but she knew she should be loving and nonjudgmental. She prayed for God to work.

As the relationship grew and Cindy felt more trust and confidence in Barbara's love and concern, she asked for advice. She knew her life was in confusion, and she knew the degree of personal pain this was causing her. She just didn't know how to find her way out. Barbara shared about Jesus and His love, forgiveness, and healing.

In a process that took years, Cindy made a commitment to Christ, got out of the lesbian relationship, and was reconciled with her husband and family. God's grace continues to provide healing as she continues to walk with Jesus. The mentoring relationship with Barbara and with other believers continues to provide the environment Cindy needs for spiritual and personal growth.

CHAPTER 12

WHAT IS IT?

As our ministry continued to grow in those early years, four essential elements of the New Life model emerged:

1. a focus on bridge-building relationships with non-Christians
2. required involvement in a small-group team
3. the required basic training course
4. larger, monthly celebration gatherings, where we focus on worshiping God

In addition to the basic training course, other New Life training courses focus on building leaders for small teams, teaching new believers the basics of walking with Jesus, and teaching parents how to disciple their children in the family context.

Seen from the perspective of fulfilling God's Great Commission (to go out, find the lost, lead them to faith, and disciple them to maturity), it was clear to us what this new approach offered: It's *relationally* driven. It provided a means to work through relationships, community, and networks of people to achieve God's objectives for us in this world—a much better strategy for today's postmodern, non-Christian culture.

CHURCH OR PARACHURCH?

Meanwhile I was often asked (and still am) if New Life is a biblical church or if it is, in fact, a parachurch ministry.

As background to my answer, it's interesting to note that parachurch ministries almost always have arisen in response to some missing function of the church—whether missions, or evangelism, or ministry to youth, collegians, prisoners, the homeless, or whomever. Groups of concerned Christians arise in obedience to God's Spirit to meet the needs being neglected by the church. When considered from this perspective, there doesn't really seem to be any such thing as a "parachurch" ministry. Perhaps these are simply parts of the church that have arisen to fill holes in the existing structure.

Consequently, we don't characterize New Life as a parachurch ministry. As our people are trained to go as cross-cultural missionaries to the unchurched around them, and as they evangelize and disciple those whom they reach, they're actually planting a new indigenous church in the midst of the secular culture. The body that grows up out of this is an indigenous product of the Holy Spirit and God's followers in a new culture, and it has what we recognize as the minimum characteristics of a biblical church (both the church universal and each local expression of it): It's the people of God, called together under the lordship of Christ, characterized by love, and committed to living out the Great Commandment.

Often when Christians from traditional model churches look at any new-paradigm church and ask, "Is this really a biblical church?" what they actually mean is, "If it doesn't have a building, a sanctuary, a pulpit, pews, or a senior pastor, how can it possibly be a biblical church?"

New Life doesn't have its own building, but that isn't a biblical requirement for a church. One of the questions we've frequently been asked is, "Where will this new church be?" Although evangelical Christians will tell you that "the church" is, in fact, the people of God and shouldn't be confused with a building or organization (a mistake often made by "liberals" and secular people), they still have difficulty envisioning the church as something other than the physical place where we meet for worship on Sunday morning. So many Christians still believe that having a building where we meet and worship is somehow core to our being a "church."

In fact, the church's building has largely become the tail that wags the dog. It's a major source of stress in terms of capacity—how can we possibly build, buy, or borrow enough space for our Sunday morning worship needs? This peak space need can have an overwhelming impact on a congregation's finances, and the lack of that space can be a major limitation to growth. If people can't get a seat or a parking space for the Sunday morning worship service, they won't join your congregation.

Churches feel guilty about having invested in expensive real estate that's used for only a few hours on Sunday, so the reaction is to try to schedule as many church activities as possible—teaching, fellowship, evangelism—in the building throughout the week. Thus we now see a seven-days-a-week philosophy of ministry that takes this real estate driven issue to its logical conclusion.

Meanwhile, rather than having form follow function, the "ministry" of God's people is distorted to try to fit into the box of the church's facility. Everything is designed to utilize the building rather than having ministry take place in the home, the neighborhood, the workplace. No wonder so many people see Christianity as "what you do at church." No wonder the laity are not empowered and acclimated to live the Christian life beyond the church building.

The early church did not have its own buildings, but that didn't seem to slow the growth of the church. For over three hundred years, the church normally met wherever the people of God gathered: houses, public buildings, even the Laundromat (the riverbank)! Only after Constantine gave the church official status—and the governing Romans mandated that religious buildings be converted into Christian churches—did the church get into the building business big time.

I suspect real estate has been a major drag on the progress of the gospel ever since. This focus clearly plays on the human tendency to put our faith in that which is visible (the building, the decorations, the relics) rather than in God, who's visible only through the eyes of faith.

LOOKING TO SCRIPTURE

James H. Rutz in *The Open Church* shows that most of our cherished church structures came from secular, pagan, or, at best, political sources rather than from the pages of the New Testament.

In his book *Radical Renewal: The Problem of Wineskins Today,* Howard A. Snyder offers a stinging critique of the structure used by most traditional model churches. He says if we were really serious about having a "biblical" or "New Testament" church, we would have to completely revamp our current forms and practices. He also states that our use of buildings alone demonstrates values that totally contradict the values required of the church in the New Testament.

Our current practice, according to Snyder, "shows that we see the church as a building and not as a living people of God." Our buildings show that we're "inflexible—unwilling and unable to change to meet the changing needs and culture around us." They indicate the lack of fellowship we experience. "They are uncomfortable and impersonal, designed for the participation of a few leaders." They highlight our pride—"showing our priorities are not people and their needs but self-glorification." Furthermore, our church buildings "promote class division by advertising the socioeconomic class we want to attract."[8]

What does the Bible tell us on the issue of church structure and forms? Leith Anderson, in *A Church for the 21st Century,* notes this:

> The New Testament is surprisingly silent about many of
> the matters we associate with church structure and life.

There's no mention of architecture, pulpits, length of typical sermons, or rules for having a Sunday School. Little
is said about the style of music, order of worship, or
times of church gatherings. There were no Bibles,
denominations, camps, pastor's conferences, or board
meetings. Those who strive to be New Testament
churches must seek to live its principles and absolutes,
not reproduce the details. We don't know many of the
details, and if we reproduced the ones we do know, we
would end up with synagogues, speaking Greek, and the
divisive sins of the Corinthians.[9]

The New Testament contains literally hundreds of passages that
directly or indirectly describe the characteristics the church is to have.
But there is no imperative command related to what the church structure or building should be. In fact, practically all the commands
addressed to the church have to do with how we relate to one another
or to God.

Those New Testament relational imperatives to the body of Christ
clearly show what we're to look like as we, the people of God, are knit
together in and by the Holy Spirit. For example, as believers we are
told to

- love one another (John 17:23; Romans 12:9-10; Ephesians
  4:1-6).
- put others before ourselves (Ephesians 4:22-30; Philippians
  2:1-4).

- follow the leading of the Spirit so that each person is building up the body (Romans 12:1-8; 1 Corinthians 12:12-26; Colossians 3:15-17).
- make allowances for differences so all can live in harmony (Romans 14:1-12; Hebrews 10:10,19-25).
- forgive one another (2 Corinthians 2:7-8; Galatians 6:1-10).
- confront, counsel, and discipline each other (2 Thessalonians 3:6-10; James 5:19-20).
- avoid immorality and wrongdoing in our lives (1 Corinthians 5:1-13; Ephesians 4:17-32).
- have a positive attitude in all we do (Philippians 2:5-18; 1 Peter 4:7-19).

WHERE CHRIST IS

I find two strong conclusions arising from all this: First, whatever structure the church assumes should be dictated by these relational imperatives addressed to the church; the form or structure should facilitate our living out all those relational demands. Second, the forms should be culturally relevant, so as not to create an obstacle to anyone in the surrounding culture and prevent them from coming to faith in Jesus Christ.

Clearly, buildings are not a requirement of a biblical church. Under the New Covenant of Jesus Christ, God now dwells not in a particular place, not in any temple or tabernacle, but in His people. The heart of incarnational theology is that He's with us, in us. Wherever two or three are gathered in Christ's name, He is there.

When people asked us, "Where will your church be located?" we responded, "Wherever the people of God are." Our ministry currently serves twenty-seven towns here in New Hampshire and in Maine, extending over a range of about forty-five minutes' drive time. One of the goals of our ministry is to train people to live and minister in the communities where God has planted them. So the functions of the ministry—friendship, training, and nurture—take place, for the most part, in natural environments such as homes, restaurants, offices, conference rooms, recreational facilities, and other similar settings, right in the communities where people live. This approach brings the church to the people rather than trying to bring the people to a church building.

Our monthly celebrations are the one ministry function for which believers from different parts of a larger region travel to one central spot. We use existing large-group function spaces for these meetings, including restaurants, conference facilities, community buildings, and school buildings.

Meanwhile, the organizational and administrative needs of our ministry are coordinated out of office space rented in a central location for the area that is being served. The telephone, e-mail, fax, and computer provide a high level of support and service to our widely scattered groups of people. Today's effective technology can provide support, communication, and information to many more people than the old "church office" could—and do it twenty-four hours a day at a much lower labor cost.

In this and previous chapters I've described several of our practices in New Life's ministry, but these are really only secondary issues. Much more important are the principles that underlie these practices and grow out of our priorities. Let's focus on these in the following chapter.

CHAPTER 13

TRANSFERABLE
PRINCIPLES

As the New Life ministry grew, word of mouth spread the good news to others who had an interest in effective strategies for reaching those outside the church. We began to receive telephone calls from people all across the country who wanted our "curriculum" so they could use it in their own communities. I told them we didn't actually know what we were doing. We were simply asking God how to reach lost people we couldn't reach through our church. We shared with one another the answers He gave us, and we tried lots of ideas. The ideas that worked, we encouraged more of. The ideas that didn't work, we simply tossed.

Over time we understood more of the why behind some of the successes and failures, and we began to get a better picture of what the Lord was up to. We kept good notes so we could pass on to others what worked and what didn't work.

PRACTICES VERSUS PRINCIPLES

Twenty years ago there were only a handful of churches in America with more than two thousand people in attendance on Sunday morning. Now there are well over four hundred. Many of us in New England have the opportunity to attend seminars or conferences where we can learn about some of the more successful and highly publicized of these megachurches. Ministry leaders from Florida or California or Illinois come to town to explain in detail their specific practices. The implication is that if we do worship or drama or prayer or Bible teaching or whatever exactly as they've done it, we'll see the same kind of success here in New England.

But it rarely, if ever, happens. I could give you lots of illustrations of well-motivated ministries in New England that staunchly copied the details of some famous ministry's practices and failed.

The reason is quite simple. There are wide regional and cultural variations among people groups across the United States. Practices that work in the suburbs of Chicago won't necessarily work in the suburbs of Boston. In fact, practices generally don't transfer very well across cultural boundaries. Principles are transferable. Practices are not.

Think about our application of New Testament truths to our lives today. We don't transfer specific practices from those pages—we transfer the principles. How effective would the church of Jesus Christ be in your community if all the believers spoke Aramaic or street Greek? Where I live in New Hampshire, Christianity would die off quickly if we all had to trudge through snow in sandals, with minus-twenty-degree winds whipping up our robes. Or if we always set out on a trip literally following Jesus' instructions to bring nothing but our "cloak."

It's the effective transfer of principles across cross-cultural barriers that leads to the successful planting of indigenous churches in new populations. We must try to shed our own cultural clothing from the gospel and replace it with new cultural clothing that fits the people group God has called us to minister to. This principle holds true in the United States as well as overseas, in transferring the principles not only from one region or city to another but also among different people groups within the same city. Bankers and bikers are two people groups I can think of who may live in the same area but require different practices to be effectively evangelized and discipled. There's no such thing as "one size fits all."

NEW LIFE PRINCIPLES

That's the reason we were so slow to respond to people who wanted to take our New Life approach and use it elsewhere. First we wanted to be sure we'd actually learned what God was trying to teach us. We wanted to be sure that we'd identified the core issues in our ministry and really knew how to make them work. Then we wanted to watch New Life in action long enough to figure out the transferable principles that underlie our local success.

We've identified the following six principles that we believe make New Life effective in reaching the culturally unchurched. These principles drive New Life and its success. We believe that if you allow the Holy Spirit to flesh them out to fit your situation and the people you're called to minister to, your ministry will be fruitful. Your practices may look quite different from ours, and that's fine. It's part of the process God uses to make the ministry fit the wide variety of people and cultures we have in the United States.

1. *The ministry is relationally driven.* People learn ministry skills and successfully translate them into their own relational worlds. The cultural traits of today's lost generations require a church that's relationally based. In an article in *Christianity Today,* William Dyrness noted that the driving need of secular people today is relational, and that they seek to understand themselves in relational terms. "No longer are they asking the question, 'How can I understand myself as an individual with purpose and meaning?'" Their question instead is, "How can I connect with others and make a difference?"[10]

2. *The ministry is highly portable.* The tools and skills are flexible and adaptable wherever you go.

3. *The ministry is lay-driven and lay-led.* Many traditional ministry approaches (both church and parachurch models) are severely limited by their need for paid professional staff. One of the major reasons for the growth of Mormonism is that it's a lay-driven, lay-led movement. Local congregations are headed by lay leaders, and even the area bishops are laymen who volunteer up to forty hours a week to this role. Compared to their Protestant counterparts, Mormon congregations have

extremely low overhead and operating costs and a very high level of lay volunteer service in ministry.

4. *The ministry has a minimum of complexity.* Most people don't have the time, even if they do have the ability, to go and learn a complex program. They need something they can quickly learn and make their own. We've tried to pare down and streamline the basics of the Christian life so laypeople will be able to carry it across the cultural boundaries to the pre-Christians in their world, where the Holy Spirit can guide in each specific application.

After all, the gospel itself is really simple. My junior-high daughter explained it to me like this: "God made us for a relationship with Him. We sinned; the price is death. Jesus paid the price on the Cross. All we have to do is accept His free gift to be connected with God." That's simple enough that even I can understand it.

5. *The ministry is mission focused.* Our mission in New Life is to reach as many people for Jesus as possible and to disciple them into mature, reproducing followers of Jesus. Everything that we do is focused on achieving those results. Compared to the typical local church, that's a very narrow focus, but it creates an environment where the Holy Spirit brings fruitfulness to the ministry.

6. *The ministry promotes full-spectrum discipleship.* Our goal is not evangelism. Our goal is to present every person mature in Christ, an objective clearly spelled out in Colossians 1:28. Evangelism is simply a point along that process.

I'm convinced the reason most Christians seldom have anyone ask them about their faith is that they simply wouldn't know how to handle it. Most Christians would get all flustered and confused and never be able to get it out. So God doesn't let the encounter take place. Only when we're prepared and ready to answer the question will God bring people into our lives to ask it. By focusing on full-spectrum discipleship, people are praying and looking for opportunities and are ready to deal with them when they come. The Holy Spirit can use this preparation and focus to produce spiritual fruitfulness.

When we focus almost exclusively on the point of conversion, it's easy to become spiritual mercenaries—simply trying to get more "convert scalps" to hang on our belt. It often leads to shortchanging the whole process of building friendships with those who are lost. It also leads to the mistaken belief that once a person has made a commitment to Christ and has come forward and prayed the prayer, then our job is done—another convert won and in the kingdom. But without effective discipleship, we simply populate the kingdom with weak infants unable to grow to maturity in Christ.

THESE PRINCIPLES IN ACTION

With these principles in mind, let me share some of the experiences of New Life people that illustrate, in different ways, these principles in action.

Sal and Betsy Vincent live in Cincinnati, Ohio. Sal has had a long career in banking, and Betsy is a hairdresser. Both are committed Christians who have been growing in their faith through a prominent local church.

Sal loves his job and certainly wouldn't want to give it up to become a full-time pastor. Most of his skills and gifts are far better suited to keeping track of banking details. He probably wouldn't enjoy or be very successful at spending his days counseling people with problems. He has often wanted to become a missionary (especially during stirring presentations in his church's annual mission conference), but he wasn't really willing to give up his day job or leave home.

Over the years Sal and Betsy's heart for reaching lost people has continued to grow, but they've struggled with how best to do that through their local church. When the church decided to plant a new congregation specifically designed to reach Boomers and Busters, Sal and Betsy were among the first to sign up. The church plant was somewhat disappointing. It simply didn't give them the chance to minister to lost people as they'd hoped.

The Vincents were part of a group from their area who approached us for help with learning the principles of New Life. Now Sal has finally had his dream come true. He's a cross-cultural missionary, but he hasn't had to give up his home in Cincinnati or his job at the bank. The bank is now his mission field.

At the same time God has provided a breakthrough for Betsy as well. She had been sensing a call to ministry and was praying and thinking about giving up her job as a hairdresser and going to work at the church. She says,

> Thanks to New Life, I now realize that God has already
> given me a full-time ministry. It has been under my hands

every day. I just didn't know it. I have people who come to me all day long. They open up. They share their fears, their failures, and their loves. I'm like a full-time counselor and with the help of New Life, now I can be a counselor for Jesus and these people He's made a part of my life. I have the relationships where God can use me in ministry. I've actually had them all along. I just didn't realize it until New Life helped me to see what God has been trying to do in my life.

Joanie is a widow in her late fifties. She became a believer about ten years ago. Since then she's always looked forward to the summers when a number of evangelical women her age would hold a weekly Christian Bible study. She enjoyed visiting with other Christian women each week as well as learning from God's Word.

Joanie lives in an exclusive gated community with about fifty lovely homes. It's a classic country club with twenty-seven holes of golf, an elegant clubhouse, a beach, and other amenities. It isn't a community where outsiders—including door-to-door salesmen or tract-bearing Christians—can gain easy entry or acceptance.

After going through our first New Life basic training course, Joanie began to pray about how to reach her pre-Christian neighbors. After much prayer and reflection, she decided to give up her summer women's Bible study and learn to play golf, which is the major summertime activity of the women in her community. As she began building bridges of friendship, some of these women began to ask her questions about the

Bible and her relationship with God. She now has a Bible study group with them, held inside the gated community.

Wendy Davis is a lovely woman in her late forties who for several years attended a strong church where she received great biblical preaching and teaching. She seemed to be a committed and consistent believer who sincerely desired to follow God.

After Wendy went through our basic training and became part of a small group, she started to open up and ask questions. She had reservations about whether she had made the step of faith and whether her salvation was secure. Through our ministry, she got a clear picture of the gospel and how to apply it in her life. She accepted Jesus, and for the first time, she was certain of her status in the kingdom.

Wendy's husband, Dave, was an on-again, off-again churchgoer from a Catholic background. As Wendy began growing in her walk with Jesus, she and her small group companions reached out in love to Dave. He made his own commitment to Jesus after about nine months of experiencing their love and commitment.

Jeb Smart was born and raised in a pastor's family. After graduation from college, he felt called to minister to kids. Using the paradigm he knew best, he went to work as a youth pastor for a church. Over the next eight years, Jeb held a number of positions in church ministry. While he kept his love for kids, he found churches to be difficult places to work. So he left the ministry and accepted a position as the recreation director for a small town.

He felt a degree of guilt and depression about not being in "full-time Christian service," but his involvement in New Life helped Jeb realize that he had a larger ministry in rec work than he ever had in the church. He was in touch with hundreds of kids each week in the schools and in after-school programs. He was in relationships with many families in the community, and the community leaders became his good friends. He saw that God had given him a tremendous ministry opportunity in which he could focus on people and real spiritual needs.

George Harris had been a junior high school teacher for thirty years and a Christian for about four when he took our basic training course. One evening during a session he was attending, I made a prediction I routinely make in the session on learning how to quickly share your story and the basic gospel. I told the group that some of them would return to our next session with the exciting report that for the first time in their Christian life, someone came up to them and asked about their faith.

As George was leaving the session, he immediately met a high-school kid who had been a student of his. "He asked what I was doing there," George recalls. "I told him I was taking some Christian training. He said, 'I would really like to hear about how you got involved in that.'"

Two weeks later, the student showed up in George's classroom after school. He said, "Mr. Harris, I really would like to hear about the Christian thing." George replied, "Sure I'd be happy to tell you about it sometime." The young man pulled up a chair in front of his desk and sat down. George said later, "I guess that was God's way of telling me that it was time to share!"

So he told the student his story, just as he had learned in our training. He also invited the young man (who was now president of the junior class in his high school) over to dinner at his home the following Friday night. Over dinner, George and his wife, Marci, shared the gospel with the student, who prayed to receive Christ. Today he's growing as a disciple who follows Jesus.

CHAPTER 14

WHAT YOU CAN DO

Chuck Mercer was an engineer and executive with one of the largest steel companies in the United States. For many years he ran one of the company's largest plants. His hard-driving personality contributed to his business success but undermined his life at home. His harshness created tension and turmoil for his wife and kids.

Chuck's wife was a committed believer; Chuck was not. But for more than twenty-five years he joined her in attending one of the strongest evangelical churches in the suburbs of Boston. The pastor, the elders, and many others in the church prayed for Chuck regularly, but nothing seemed to penetrate his hardened heart.

Eventually one of the elders told the pastor that they weren't going to pray for Chuck anymore. "We've never seen anyone so far from the Lord or so resistant to God's love," he said. It seemed that God would never be able to reach him.

Chuck retired and moved up to New Hampshire where he'd owned a lake cottage for many years. One day he "bumped" into Carol, a woman who had been in his third grade elementary school class in Arlington, Massachusetts. She and her husband had also retired in the Lakes Region. They had a pleasant conversation standing there on the street, and Carol invited Chuck to try out the small Congregational church she was part of in a nearby town. Chuck and his wife did so, and after the first Sunday, he asked his wife if they could go again. The second Sunday he sat quietly through the service with tears running down his cheeks. He went home that day and gave his life to Jesus Christ. God had spoken to him of His love and forgiveness in such a compelling way that Chuck wanted nothing else but to walk with Jesus for the rest of his life.

God's love transformed him. Those who knew the old Chuck—even his wife and children—could hardly believe this gentle, loving, compassionate, and considerate man was the same person.

The lesson in that story: *Never give up!* As long as someone is alive, it's never too late for God to reach that person with His love and forgiveness. God cares for every lost person more deeply than we would care for our own children if they were lost and at risk. We may be inclined to give up on those who seem hardened, but God hasn't given up and never will. He's the God of love, of perseverance, and of action. His love and faithfulness can overcome the hardest situations and reach people whom most of us would write off as unreachable.

THE PEOPLE ON YOUR MIND

Let me ask you a question. As you've been reading this book, have certain people come to mind? People you know and care about, who don't yet know Jesus? Or perhaps people whose progress in their journey of faith you're unsure about? Perhaps God is laying these people on your heart because He wants to use you in some way to help them come into a relationship with Jesus.

Take a moment now and ask God how He might be able to reach these people through you. Remember, it's not you who has to reach them. That's the Holy Spirit's job. If God uses you, it will be by building a bridge of friendship that the Spirit can work through.

Ask God to speak to you. Have a pen and blank sheet of paper handy. Jot down what God says as you wait on Him. Record any person's name He brings to mind. Don't worry at this point about how "good" a prospect anyone is. God often calls the most unlikely people into the kingdom. Sometimes the "nice" people who seem closest to a "Christian lifestyle" are the hardest to reach, while those who seem farthest from God are the most open to Him.

My dear friend Kyle Bloom had a difficult childhood, and by his early teens he had a significant drinking problem. By his early twenties he was an alcoholic and had other drug addictions as well. He eventually found help through Alcoholics Anonymous and other support groups. Yet he seemed like a pretty tough case for the gospel—inward, self-sufficient, cynical, suspicious, and not inclined to trust.

One day I asked him how it was that he ever became a Christian. He answered, "My wife was a believer, and I figured my two daughters would be, too. When I thought about eternity, I just couldn't imagine spending it in some place other than where my wife and girls were. I wanted to be with them, so I accepted Jesus." God can bring the most unlikely people through the most unlikely means.

YOUR QUALIFICATIONS

You may not feel qualified to be used by God to help reach another person. Most of us don't. We tend to be aware of the problems, the weaknesses, and the sin in our lives, and we feel these things disqualify us from being used by God. Nothing could be further from the truth. Being aware of your failings and shortcomings simply qualifies you as a member of the human race. We all as believers have a mixture of the "old man" and the "new man" in us, and those two parts are at war every day. In His grace, God chooses to use us in spite of our sinfulness. In fact, He says that His power is made complete when He works through our weakness.

Trust me, if God can work through *me,* given my struggles with the old nature, then He can work through anybody. He doesn't choose to work through us because we deserve it. He does so out of love and compassion for the lost and for us, His dearly beloved children. Don't try to understand it. Just accept it and step out in faith. God can and will use you to love others to Him in spite of your condition, if you let Him.

You may not have had much success in sharing your faith in the past. Or you may have had a number of really bad experiences that turned you off on the whole notion of sharing your faith. My advice: *Don't give up!* God wants you to experience the exhilaration of sharing your faith with others and seeing the Holy Spirit transform their lives. This is a vital part of the abundant life Jesus promises to those who love and follow Him.

Remember my early flying career? It wasn't that God didn't want me to fly. The bed sheet and the leap off the cinderblocks were simply the wrong way to get there. If you've experienced some failure in sharing your faith, consider it a good education. Now that you know some methods that don't work, get up, dust yourself off, and move on to find methods that God can use to help you share your faith effectively.

TAKING IT PERSONALLY

If this whole issue is becoming a bit personal for you because of how much you care for certain people, good! I believe God wants us to share out of love and concern for others. I'm not sure that witnessing out of a sense of obligation or duty counts for much with God. And I suspect that lost people can tell the difference between genuine love and concern and a sense of obligation to collect spiritual brownie points. I doubt that anything other than genuine love and sincere concern carries weight with pre-Christians.

As you pray and God puts people on your mind, begin to pray also that He'll open up opportunities to begin building friendships that have spiritual potential.

Then get to know the people He's brought into your life better. Do things together that give you common experiences. Develop a level of communication and trust in your relationship. Pray that God would open times when you can talk about spiritual issues.

Be prepared to share your own story of faith. Practice answering the question, "What difference does knowing Jesus make in my life?" Be prepared to explain the gospel in a way that's simple, clear, and easy to act on. Be ready to work with the Holy Spirit as He helps your friend make the spiritual transaction that leads to a commitment to Jesus.

Finally, be prepared and willing to walk side by side with your friend, helping him or her grow in faith to attain spiritual maturity. (This last step often takes several years or longer.)

All of this is much easier to learn and implement if you don't do it alone. If you can, find someone else to do it with you. You may be thinking, "But I really don't know how to do those things. No one has ever shown me how." That's okay. Most people in the church find themselves in the same situation. For help, you can contact us at the address in the back of this book and ask for resources that can make learning these skills easier.

JOINING OTHERS

Do you have a group of friends who have a concern for lost people? Then consider working together to start a ministry like ours to the culturally unchurched in your community. What does it take to start? It's really pretty simple. (I'd call our ministry "Christianity for Dummies," but some of my associates take offense at that phrase.) The truth is, if you can read, if you love the Lord and have a heart for lost people, you can start a ministry like ours. You really don't need a Bible school degree or a seminary diploma. All you need are a handful of friends who are concerned about lost family, friends, and neighbors who are outside the reach of the local church.

Here are some foundational steps you can take:

I recommend that you put aside your thoughts about your current church situation and structure. Forget everything you know about "how" to live the Christian life, especially how to live it with others. Give God your mind as a blank page and start from scratch. "Be transformed by the renewing of your mind" (Romans 12:2). To be able to hear and follow God into the adventure of forging a new paradigm for sharing the gospel, we all need something of the childlikeness Jesus praised in Luke 18:15-17.

If you try to start such a ministry inside your church (to prop up a failing structure), I'm convinced it will fail. Even if your church is healthy, a ministry like New Life is designed to reach the people whom your church *can't* reach.

You don't really need a church to start a ministry like this. Of course, a church could sponsor the start of such a ministry to reach those who are outside its reach. That's how we got started, and it makes a lot of sense for several reasons.

A church, like any organization, has limits to the degree to which it can be stretched. This concept I call "cultural elasticity." If you try to introduce too much change too soon, the resulting level of discomfort and upheaval may well trigger the loss of the church's core people—the 20 percent who provide 80 percent of the church's finances, workers, and leadership. It makes more sense to start a focused ministry to the lost as a separate missionary outreach and to keep the church's current people group intact.

When Jesus spoke of the shepherd who went out to find the one lost sheep, notice that he didn't pick up the sheepfold and move it to where the lost one was. Instead, he left the ninety-nine safely in the fold as he went out on his search. In the same way, we believe God is calling together mission teams who will leave the comfort of their present church and go out in a special effort to find those who are beyond the reach of the traditional church. Rather than being immersed in the culture dominated by church activities and relationships, such teams will build bridges of friendship into the cultures of the lost.

I'm often asked this question: "But once you've reached new converts, why wouldn't you simply incorporate them into the church?" Assuming that you actually *could* overcome the cultural barriers and that one of these converts from an unchurched culture could be effectively discipled in the traditional church—it would be self-defeating to do so. You would create a "hybrid Christian." A plant grown from hybrid seeds crossbred from two standard plant varieties will typically bloom for only one generation. It isn't able to reproduce itself. Likewise, once you've brought converts from the unchurched culture into the traditional church, you've probably destroyed their future potential for reaching others from their background. In essence you've only created more "sterile Christians," with which the church is already over-populated.

This would be like requiring missionaries sent overseas to ship all their new converts back to America to be discipled and trained to maturity. This strategy might be beneficial in some ways for these converts, but it obviously would severely limit their ability to reach their own indigenous cultures for Christ. This is the same error the "Judaizers" made in the Christian church of the first century. They simply didn't see how a Gentile could really become a follower of Jesus without adopting all the cultural standards of orthodox Judaism.

Jesus spoke to this when He said,

> And no one pours new wine into old wineskins. If he does, the new wine will burst the skins, the wine will run out and the wineskins will be ruined. No, new wine must be poured into new wineskins. And no one after drinking old wine wants the new, for he says, "The old is better." (Luke 5:37-39)

THE ROLE OF THE TRADITIONAL MODEL CHURCH

The traditional model church still has an important role to play in God's economy. The point I make is that we shouldn't confuse its role with that of the new-paradigm church. When pastors, church leaders, and congregations are ineffective, it's usually because they're struggling to be somebody else rather than discovering and accepting the gifts and mission God has given them. Any church can succeed at evangelism and discipleship—if it's based on God's design for that church. If we have an accurate and honest understanding of our spiritual gifts and our call as a congregation, God can help us find our appropriate ministry style to take advantage of today's opportunities.

The key issue is to honestly identify the characteristics of our congregations' culture as well as the spiritual gifts of our church leadership.

If you feel most comfortable in a traditional model church, by all means stay with it. God can and will use these kind of churches to reach more people for Christ. He may yet reform the traditional model church in some way we cannot yet see, just as He has inspired reforms in churches in the past.

While hoping for the best, you might also keep an open mind about church form and structure. Today's new-paradigm churches may look a bit like lifeboats floating next to the grand and glorious Titanic—the traditional model church. But if this enormous edifice begins slipping beneath the waves of cultural change, those lifeboats will start looking quite attractive. You—or more likely your children or grandchildren—will wish you had one. So keep an open mind about what form the church may take in the future and how our God (who's always full of good surprises) may act to lead people to Jesus. Many of those you love and care about may find salvation through new-paradigm churches in the future.

Meanwhile, life goes on. God continues to call each of us to go out and search for the lost children who are in the woods all around us.

RESEARCH YOUR COMMUNITY AND RELATIONAL NETWORKS

In addition to deciding how such a ministry to the culturally un-churched will impact your own current church situation, another big step is researching your community and your relational networks.

With a clear mind-set and with your friends who share your heart for reaching the lost, take paper and pen and ask the following questions:

- What is our community like?
- What's the economic base?
- What distinct neighborhoods can we identify?
- What kinds of people live here?
- Can we identify distinct groups or types of people?
- Where do these various groups hang out or spend their time?
- What do they do for recreation and fun?

In as much detail as you can, describe the local people group or groups you think you might want to reach. And ask yourself, What does my own relational network look like? Who are the relatives, friends, coworkers, classmates, neighbors, or others with whom I have a relationship? Try to cast the net as broadly as you can. They might be people you see daily, weekly, a couple of times a month, or even once a year—but you know them and they know you. The potential is there to build deeper relationships, if God should lead and some effort is invested.

Thinking about these people you know, what are your best opportunities to connect with them? How might you be in a situation to have a relaxed and natural conversation with them? What kinds of things do you currently have in common? What other common experiences might you share together?

Then you can prayerfully begin to act on what you've learned and what God shows you.

While searching the people networks God has already built into your life, you and a handful of friends with a heart for lost people can together provide yourselves with both the training and community to effectively reach lost people. (Again, if you contact us, our New Life Center has resources to help you.)

DO IT

Whatever you do, *don't make the mistake of continuing to live a Christian life that's only business as usual.* Jesus tells the story of a rich young man in Matthew 19. The young man confirmed for Jesus all the right things he'd done in pursuit of eternal life. Jesus said in essence, "You're on the right track; now go sell your possessions and give to the poor." Afraid to move out of his personal comfort zone (wealth), this young man "went away sad."

Jesus then told His followers, "Everyone who has left houses or brothers or sisters or father or mother or children or fields for my sake will receive a hundred times as much and will inherit eternal life" (verse 29). The cost at times may seem high—but it's always insignificant compared to the rewards.

So whatever you do, don't just sit there—*do* something!

STUDY AND DISCUSSION GUIDE

The following questions can be used for an individual study of *The Jesus Plan* or as a guide to studying and discussing the book in a group setting.

CHAPTER 1: LOST

1. In what ways does your own past experience help you understand the lostness of today's unbelievers?

2. In what ways might your own past experience be a hindrance to fully understanding the lostness of today's unbelievers?

3. In your own life story, what circumstances and events led up to your search for meaning in life and for spiritual reality and truth?

4. What helped you most to understand and believe the gospel of Christ?

5. The author writes, "My conversion was divine intervention. God was going to get hold of my life regardless. His grace, pure and simple—no other explanation does justice to it." Can you make the same statement about your own conversion? Why or why not?

6. The author uses the label "errors of direction" to describe his youthful attempts "to find purpose in life from secular values, art, and education." Then he adds that these are "the kinds of choices that continue to be not only socially acceptable but also strongly promoted by American culture as valid guideposts for the journey through life." Do you agree or disagree with the author's assessment on this point? Explain your answer.

7. A key point made by the author is that "Even Christians seem confused at times about the difference between religion and a relation-

ship with Jesus. Far too often we've exchanged the life-giving personal relationship with our Lord and Savior for a sorry mess of lifeless religious traditions and nonsense." Do you think this problem as identified by the author is serious and widespread? Why or why not?

CHAPTER 2: TWO HUNDRED MILLION

1. The author says that millions of Americans today are "lost not only spiritually but in many other ways. They're relationally lost.… They're emotionally and psychologically lost.… They're lost in terms of having no sense of community.…" Is *lost* the same word you would use to describe what you see in these different aspects of secular American life and culture today? Why or why not?

2. Think about how many people you come in personal contact with on a typical day in your life. How many of these people would you estimate are spiritually lost, as the author uses that term?

3. Of the unbelievers you know, can you think of some who, as the author states, "realize they're lost, and if they knew how to get out of the woods and find God, they would act on that knowledge"? If so, how did you reach that conclusion about them?

4. Can you think of others who, as the author says, "aren't even aware they're lost"? What evidence leads you that conclusion?

5. Do you know some people whose situation and circumstances are much like those of Jason Patterson, the man whose story is given as an example in this chapter? In what ways are these people you know like Jason?

6. The author declares, "Lost people matter to God!" What convinces you most—from Scripture or otherwise—that this statement is true?

7. Do you ever find yourself feeling that lost people do *not* matter to God? If so, what factors influence your thinking in that direction?

8. Look at the three parables Jesus told in Luke 15. Try to read them with a fresh pair of eyes. As you read them this time, what words or images or thoughts stand out to you most as a statement of God's love for the lost?

9. The author says, "We need to pray that God will break our hearts and our proud spirits that we might see these two hundred million lost souls in the same way He does." Do you agree that this is what we "need" to do? If so, how and when can you pray this prayer? And who can pray it with you?

10. The author asks, "So what exactly should our action be?" Examine for yourself the Scriptures which the author then refers to: Matthew

10:1,5; Luke 10:1-2; Matthew 28:18-19; and Acts 1:8. What words or images or thoughts stand out to you most in these verses as a guide for what our action should be toward unbelievers?

11. "The conclusion," writes the author, "is inescapable. *We must be willing to go out and search for the lost* so that God can redeem them. God Himself is asking—no, commanding—those of us who love Him to go out into the dark night and comb the woods until these lost ones are found and brought in to the family of God." Do you agree with the author on this point? Why or why not?

12. Listen again to the author's final words in this chapter: "The purpose of this book is to help us examine our assumptions about the world we live in today and determine how to go about accomplishing what God has called us to do as Christians. We need to be open to the Lord and examine the evidence to see if our assumptions are correct. If, in fact, they are not, we have to trust that God can show us new, more effective ways to be His channels of salvation in the lost world

to which He's sent us." Use these words and thoughts as a guide for your own prayer before God, as you ask Him to lead you in your study of this book. Write your prayer or thoughts here.

CHAPTER 3: THEY AREN'T COMING IN

1. How would you summarize and evaluate your own experience of church involvement throughout your life?

2. How would you summarize and evaluate your experience of asking unbelievers to come to church with you? If you've tried it, how successful has that strategy been in winning these people to Christ?

3. Review the biographical sketches in the section titled "Meet Some of My Friends." What likenesses do you see between people you know and the people described in this section?

4. What is your understanding of America's religious situation as depicted in the survey research cited in this chapter?

5. What is your understanding of the terms "culturally un-churched" and "culturally churched" as they're used by the author?

6. From your own observations and conversations with unbelievers, what seem to be the most common reasons why people choose not to go to church? How do these reasons compare with the reasons mentioned by the author in this chapter?

CHAPTER 4: GIVING CHURCH A TRY

1. In your own life story, what was it like for you as a new Christian? What opportunities for growing spiritually did you have? What

spiritual nurturing or assistance did you have from more mature believers?

2. What situations or events in the author's experience as a new Christian stand out most to you? How would you summarize his experience as a growing Christian?

3. From your own experience and from what you see in the author's experience, what do think are the most important factors for the successful spiritual growth of a new Christian?

4. The author writes, "As a student of the Bible, I recognized the pivotal role the church plays in God's plans for mankind and the world." How would you summarize what that role is for the church in God's plans for mankind and the world?

5. The author then adds, "At the same time, I continued to find my church experience quite difficult. As I got more and more involved in the local church, I had a hard time finding people there who shared my compassion for the lost souls outside the church." Does the author's experience parallel your own? Explain your answer.

6. Do you agree that it's hard to find many people in our churches who have compassion for the lost souls outside the church? Why or why not?

7. Listen again to these key statements from the author:

"For the most part other church members seemed caught up with their own marriages and families, their work, and perhaps a few friends from church. Most evaluated their church in terms of meeting personal needs and the needs of their families, while giving little thought to the spiritually lost who surrounded them. In response to this expectation, the ministries and programs of the church were primarily directed at meeting the needs of those who were already part of the church family."

"Most churches seemed to have a largely inward focus. Their priorities and commitments usually provided a lot of services for those already in the church. Even if there had been a genuine interest in going out to reach lost people, most members were so busy in their involvement with the church's major programs that they simply had no time left for outsiders."

Consider carefully all the points made in these statements. Does the author's assessment match your own observations of the churches you've been a part of? Why or why not?

CHAPTER 5: STILL SEARCHING

1. In debates with his friend, the author's position was that "the church's primary purpose was to reach lost people, lead them to Christ, and help them grow to maturity in Him." At that time, his friend countered with this position: "The primary purpose of the church is to nurture those who are in it. Our job as church leaders is to equip the saints for the work of ministry." Whose side would you be on in this debate? What are your thoughts about the church's primary purpose?

2. From the author's involvement in the business world as well as his continuing experience with churches, what situations or events stand out most to you? How would you summarize what he was learning?

3. The author observed that churches that share his theological beliefs "are not usually good places to take seekers. They tend to want to run a doctrinal purity test on every new person who walks through the door. This approach usually doesn't work too well for a person who has no doctrine at all but is only curious to learn about Jesus." Has this been true in your own experience with churches? Explain.

4. The author concluded that "church was just not a safe or helpful environment when it came to reaching out to lost people." Is this also the conclusion you've reached? Why or why not?

5. How would you summarize the three steps involved in the strategy the author developed for evangelism in New England? And how would you evaluate the potential effectiveness for that strategy, from your own perspective? Do you think such a plan would be effective in the state or region where you live? Why or why not?

CHAPTER 6: WE AREN'T GOING OUT

1. The author asks, "Is there hope for the hundreds of millions who are spiritually lost in America today? Can they realistically expect to be intensively searched for by those who alone are able to rescue them— those who would 'tear the world apart' to find the lost?" How does the author answer these questions? And how would you answer them?

2. How would you summarize the "principle of incarnational theology" as it's referred to in this chapter?

3. Jesus said, "I will build my church; and the gates of hell shall not prevail against it" (Matthew 16:18, KJV). What is your understanding of this statement as it relates to the church's ability to reach the lost? And what is the author's understanding of this statement?

4. "The bad news," says the author, "is that the church in the West, especially in America, is not doing well." Do you agree with the author's assessment? Why or why not? What factors influence your opinion on this?

5. What factors lead the author to conclude that the church in America is "spiritually sterile"?

6. The author addresses the perception that "people in our post-Christian, postmodern secular culture are so much more resistant to the gospel than people were in the past." On what basis does the author question this claim? In your own perspective, how true do you think this claim is? Why?

7. What is the "myth of trickle-down evangelism" that the author exposes? Why does he believe it's a myth rather than reality? From your own observation, do you see some valid effectiveness to the process that the author terms "trickle-down evangelism"? If so, explain.

8. The author expresses his conviction that "God is going to have to intervene in order to change our patterns and paradigms so that we can break out of this backwater and become all that He means us to be." Is this also your own conviction? Do you think God agrees with this as well? Explain your responses.

9. "To so many of us," the author writes, "the whole notion of evangelism and witnessing eventually seems so wildly undoable that it causes us real discomfort, and even guilt and fear, to even consider it." Has this been true in your own experience? Explain.

10. On what basis does the author question the effectiveness of bringing people in to hear evangelistic speakers? of door-to-door or in-the-mall evangelism? of simply copying whatever programs the big successful churches are using?

11. What is the difference between evangelism as a gift and evangelism as a calling?

12. Do you agree with the author's assertion that "all believers are called to be witnesses for Christ"? Why or why not?

13. How does the author state the difference between evangelism and witnessing?

14. "Relationships are the most powerful way in which people today are reached and changed," the author says. "Approaches that don't reflect this truth simply don't work well anymore." If you agree with this statement, in what way(s) is it reflected in your relationships and in your effectiveness in witnessing for Christ to the unbelievers you know?

CHAPTER 7: THE ISSUE GETS PERSONAL

1. From the parts of his story narrated in this chapter, what lessons do you see the author learning?

2. The author passes along an observation made by a friend: "The biblical mandate is to have low behavioral expectations for the unsaved while holding believers accountable to high standards. But most churches seem to have reversed this." To what extent have you seen this to be true? Explain your answer.

3. In the author's continuing spiritual journey as described in this chapter, what situations or events stand out most to you? How would you summarize the lessons he was learning?

4. How would you summarize the life experiences of the author's friend, Dave Morgan, as they're described in this chapter? What lessons was he learning?

5. What did the author and his friend Dave learn from reading the book *Church Without Walls* by Jim Petersen?

CHAPTER 8: GOD'S SOLUTION

1. What three summary points does the author make in stating "American Christianity's problem" as explored so far in this book?

2. How would you summarize the biblical and historical support that the author gives for his assertion that God frequently changes the patterns and strategies He uses in His work of redeeming mankind?

3. The author paints a scenario of God's responsive action in order to "bring His unchanging redemption to people in fresh and relevant ways." How committed do you think God is to doing things "in fresh and relevant ways"? Explain your answer.

4. The author draws this conclusion: "Today, we too must be willing to leave behind our own culture and forms and comfort zones to go to the lost. Our goal is never to extract non-Christians out of their culture and pull them into ours, where they can be 'Christians like us.' Our goal is rather to plant an indigenous church—one that's culturally relevant—in that particular people group." How would you evaluate your own willingness to pursue this course of action, with this goal in mind?

5. What impresses you most in the descriptions of "new-paradigm ministries" in this chapter?

6. The author cites three important characteristics that new-paradigm ministries tend to have in common. What are they? How do they relate to the characteristics of churches or ministries that you've been involved in?

CHAPTER 9: TURNING POINT

1. In this chapter, the author's continuing spiritual journey comes to a climax. How would you summarize what happened in his life, and what was especially significant about the way it happened?

2. "The more we began to look at our world from God's perspective," the author writes, "the more we began to see our situation in a new light. The more we thought and prayed about the problem we'd identified, the more personal the issue became." Has this also been

true in your own thoughts about reaching unbelievers? Has the issue become genuinely personal for you? Explain.

3. Think of the unbelievers you know and care about most. How would you evaluate your effectiveness in the past in sharing your faith with them?

4. As you think about and pray for these people, how would you express your own personal responsibility, before God, for their spiritual condition?

5. As the author and his friend asked God to show them what to do in order to reach the lost people in their lives, in what specific ways did God respond?

6. As the author and his friend talked with others about what they were learning, he says they found that "people were more than willing to

take responsibility for individuals God had placed in their lives, if only someone would teach them what to do." Are you fully convinced that God can teach you how to work with Him in order to reach out with Jesus' love to these unbelievers whom you care most about? Why or why not?

7. The author describes five "basic skills" that he says are needed for believers to be effective missionaries to their friends. What are these skills?

8. How would you evaluate your current level of ability in nurturing and developing your own relationship with God?

9. How would you evaluate your current level of ability in dealing with issues of culture as they're described in this chapter?

10. How would you evaluate your current level of ability in building effective relationships with others?

11. How would you evaluate your current level of ability in sharing your faith with someone else?

12. How would you evaluate your current level of ability in nurturing a new believer?

CHAPTER 10: PRIORITIES DO MATTER

1. For a church or ministry or even for an individual Christian, the author indicates that *priorities* are more important than principles or practices. To what extent do you agree with this assessment and why?

2. For whatever ministry you're currently involved in, through your church or otherwise, how would you answer these questions:

What's really essential to our faith?

What should we do first?

What should we do best?

Who are we trying to impress?

Who are we trying to make comfortable?

3. The author in this chapter explains the traditional church model as contrasted with what he calls the "New Life" model. What are the differences between these two models? Which model more closely matches the priorities of the church or ministry you're involved in now?

4. How does Acts 2:42 support the traditional model of a church's priorities?

5. How does Matthew 28:19-20 support the "New Life" model of a church's priorities?

6. How would you answer this question from the author: "If your sanc-tuary burned down, how long would it take your church to find an alternate place to hold Sunday worship services?"

7. How would you answer this question from the author: "If evangelism didn't happen in your church, how long would it take for people to get upset and finally do something about it?"

8. How would you evaluate your church's effectiveness in permeating its boundaries and developing relationships between churchgoers and those on the outside?

CHAPTER 11: PROVEN IMPACT

1. What stands out to you most in the stories told in this chapter?

2. How would you assess your own level of desire and willingness to be
a part of a ministry like the one described in this chapter?

3. For what reasons did the author's New Life ministry begin attaching
so much importance to small groups? And what various functions do
these small groups serve in this ministry?

Chapter 12: What Is It?

1. The author describes "four essential elements of the New Life
model" that emerged in the early years of New Life's ministry. What
were these four elements?

2. What do you think are the advantages of a relationally driven
ministry as described in this chapter?

3. After reading this chapter's discussion of "Church or Parachurch?" what would you say are the essential elements of a biblical church?

4. What biblical passages do you consider to be most important in telling us what the church should look like? What do these passages teach us in this regard?

5. The author lists some of the New Testament's "relational imperatives to the body of Christ," then concludes that "whatever structure the church assumes should be dictated by these relational imperatives addressed to the church; the form or structure should facilitate our living out all those relational demands." Do you agree with the author's conclusion? Why or why not? Are there also other factors that should "dictate" the church's structure? What are they?

6. Look again at New Testament relational imperatives listed in this chapter; you may also want to think of others you know from Scripture. As

you think about letting these commands "dictate" your church's structure, what conclusions and questions come to mind?

CHAPTER 13: TRANSFERABLE PRINCIPLES

1. Explain in your own words the main point the author is making in the "Practices Versus Principles" section of this chapter.

2. In this chapter the author lists six principles "that we believe make New Life effective in reaching the culturally unchurched.... We believe that if you allow the Holy Spirit to flesh them out to fit your situation and the people you're called to minister to, your ministry will be fruitful."

   Principle 1: "The ministry is relationally driven." As you think and pray, how do you think this principle can be better applied to your situation?

   Principle 2: "The ministry is highly portable." How do you think this can be better applied to your ministry situation?

Principle 3: "The ministry is lay-driven and lay-led." How can this be better applied to your situation?

Principle 4: "The ministry has a minimum of complexity." How can this be better applied to your situation?

Principle 5: "The ministry is mission focused." How can this principle be better applied to your situation?

Principle 6: "The ministry promotes full-spectrum discipleship." Again, as you think and pray, how do you think this principle can be better applied to your situation?

3. This chapter concludes with stories of how these principles are put into action in the New Life ministry. What stands out to you most from these stories?

CHAPTER 14: WHAT YOU CAN DO

1. What are the key steps that the author outlines in this chapter as an appropriate response to this book's message?

2. The author asks, "As you've been reading this book, have certain people come to mind? People you know and care about, who don't yet know Jesus? Or perhaps people whose progress in their journey of faith you're unsure about? Perhaps God is laying these people on your heart because He wants to use you in some way to help them come into a relationship with Jesus." How do you respond to this?

3. The author then suggests, "Take a moment now and ask God how He might be able to reach these people through you. Remember, it's not you who has to reach them. That's the Holy Spirit's job. If God uses you, it will be by building a bridge of friendship that the Spirit can work through. Ask God to speak to you. Have a pen and blank sheet of paper handy. Jot down what God says as you wait on Him. Record any person's name He brings to mind." What encouragement do these guidelines give you? Follow these guidelines to help you explore what God would have you do.

4. Do you ever feel unqualified for being used by God to reach others with the gospel? How would you summarize the author's response to this feeling?

5. "As you pray and God puts people on your mind," the author writes, "begin to pray also that He'll open up opportunities to begin building friendships that have spiritual potential." What is your level of commitment to doing this?

6. Are you prepared to share your own story of faith? In a way that is simple and clear, explain what difference knowing Jesus has made in your life.

7. What other believers do you know who can join you in reaching out to the lost in this new and effective way?

8. The author advises that you *not* try to start such a ministry inside your church. He writes, "I recommend that you put aside your thoughts about your current church situation and structure. Forget

everything you know about "how" to live the Christian life, especially how to live it with others. Give God your mind as a blank page and start from scratch." What are the author's reasons for recommending this? Do you agree with his assessment? Explain.

9. The author writes that we should not confuse the role of the traditional model church with the role of the new-paradigm church. What does he mean by this? What are the proper roles of each one?

10. The author also advises that you research your community and your relational networks. How would you answer these questions:

What is our community like?

What's the economic base?

What distinct neighborhoods can we identify?

What kinds of people live here?

Can we identify distinct groups or types of people?

Where do these various groups hang out or spend their time?

What do they do for recreation and fun?

What does my own relational network look like?

Who are the relatives, friends, coworkers, classmates, neighbors, or others with whom I have a relationship?

11. At this point, what are your best answers to the following questions:

Thinking about the people you know, what are your best opportunities to connect with them?

What opportunities might you have to carry on a relaxed and natural conversation with them?

What kinds of things do you currently have in common?

What other common experiences might you share together?

12. What steps can you take to act on what you've learned and on what God is showing you?

13. The author's final appeal is this: "Whatever you do, don't make the mistake of continuing to live a Christian life that's only business as usual." What is your response to this exhortation?

Notes and Bibliography

1. George Barna, from Barna Research Online, http://216.87.179.136/cgi-bin. Copyright ©1999–2000 Barna Research, Ltd. (http://www.barna.org).

2. George Barna, *The Barna Report: What Americans Believe: An Annual Survey of Values and Religious Views in the United States* (Glendale, Calif.: Regal Books, 1991), 182-7.

3. "Spiritual Beliefs and the Dying Process." Gallup poll conducted by the George Gallup International Institute, 1997. Report is available on the Cummings Foundation Web site: http://www.ncf.org/reports/health.html.

4. "The Unchurched American Study," conducted by Bruno & Ridgeway Research Associates for the American Bible Society, May 1997.

5. Gary Paulsen, *Hatchet* (New York: Simon & Schuster, 1996), 47.

6. George Barna, *Today's Pastors* (Ventura, Calif.: Gospel Light, 1993), 47-8.

7. Gary Smalley, "Keys to Loving Relationships" video series, 1994 (http://www.parable.com/smalley).

8. Howard A. Snyder, *Radical Renewal: The Problem of Wineskins Today* (Houston: Touch Publications, 1996), 69-73.

9. Leith Anderson, *A Church for the 21st Century* (Minneapolis: Bethany House, 1992), 62. Used by permission.

10. William Dyrness, "Can Americans Still Hear the Good News," *Christianity Today* (April 7, 1997): 35.

The following publications are recommended for your further reading:

Anderson, Leith. *Dying for Change.* Minneapolis: Bethany House, 1990.

Barker, Joel Arthur. *Paradigms: The Business of Discussing the Future.* New York: HarperBusiness, 1992.

Celek, Tim, and Dieter Zander. *Inside the Soul of a New Generation.* Grand Rapids: Zondervan, 1995.

Cho, Paul Yonggi, Dr. *Successful Home Cell Groups.* South Plainfield, N.J.: Bridge Publishing, 1981.

Downs, Tim. *Finding Common Ground.* Chicago: Moody, 1999.

George, Carl F. *Prepare Your Church for the Future.* Tarrytown, N.Y.: Revell, 1991.

Hale, J. Russell. *The Unchurched: Who They Are and Why They Stay Away.* San Francisco: Harper & Row, 1977.

Hunter III, George G. *How to Reach Secular People.* Nashville: Abingdon, 1992.

Hybels, Lynne and Bill. *Rediscovering Church.* Grand Rapids: Zondervan, 1995.

Kennedy, John W. "Mormons on the Rise," *Christianity Today,* 15 June 1998.

Mitchell, Arnold. *The Nine American Lifestyles.* New York: Macmillan, 1983.

Newbigin, Lesslie. *The Gospel in a Pluralistic Society.* Grand Rapids: Eerdmans, 1989.

Ogden, Greg. *The New Reformation.* Grand Rapids: Zondervan, 1990.

Petersen, Jim. *Church Without Walls: Moving Beyond Traditional Boundaries.* Colorado Springs, Colo.: NavPress 1992.

Robinson, Martin, Dr. *The Faith of the Unbeliever.* Crowborough, U.K.: Monarch, 1994.

———. *To Win the West.* Crowborough, U.K.: Monarch, 1996.

Rutz, James H. *The Open Church.* Beaumont, Tex.: The SeedSowers, 1992.

Wright, Linda Raney. *Christianity's Crisis in Evangelism.* Gresham, Oreg.: Vision House, 1995.

Zurkel, C. Wayne. *Growing the Small Church.* Elgin, Ill.: Cook, 1982.

About New Life

New Life is a new-paradigm church designed to reach people who are outside the reach of the traditional model church.

I've been part of the team that developed New Life ministries, along with Dave Morgan, Steve and Christie Bravo, and Peter and Allison Balentine. We've trained and launched groups of New Life missionaries in the Lakes Region of New Hampshire and helped start other independent New Life ministries throughout New England and in Alabama, Ohio, Maryland, New York, Pennsylvania, and Washington.

From the beginning, we've seen growth from conversion evangelism of around 30 percent per year—not because we labor where people are unusually open to the gospel or because we work with Christians who are in some way exceptionally talented, but because our people are actively "searching the woods" for lost people. God, through His grace, regularly leads us to find them and bring them into His family.

Please feel free to contact us for more information or for resources to assist you in developing such a ministry in your own community.

New Life Center, Inc.
P.O. Box 712
16 Elm Street
Wolfeboro, New Hampshire 03894
(603) 569-6330
(603) 569-8469 (fax)
newlife@worldpath.net
Bruce Dreisbach, Executive Director